Praise for 'Am I *Catholic*?'

"This is a remarkable example of how grace can work in the heart of each of us when we least expect it. Kendra's story is as honest as it is inspiring, and it made me realize how easy it is to get caught up in daily concerns at the expense of our spiritual lives."

Reverend Jacek Junak, C.R.

"Kendra's story is very engaging, humorous and blunt at times. It is a quick and easy read as she witnesses to God's gentle and patient mercy."

Father James Parker

"I am not a big fan of reading, but I sat down and didn't move until I read the last page. Kendra is honest and shares all the obstacles along her journey. She swayed my brain in so many directions and inspired me to create *my LIST!* Her story was enlightening, inspirational and most importantly easy to read. Keep up your amazing faith, I can't wait to hear where it takes you next!"

Lisa Ellie

"I really enjoyed reading this book. It is an easy read, and I found Kendra's story fascinating! I hope as she continues along on her journey, she continues to write, as her shared story could help others find their way 'home' to their Catholic faith."

Frances I. Plante

"Kendra gives a touching and unfiltered account of how her life has been transformed and empowered through a reconnection with her faith. Her story is one that many can relate to and her courage to transition from the "C-Suite" to "God's Suite" by helping others enrich their life through faith and prayer is truly inspirational."

Jeff C. Baker, Founder, Dreambridge Coaching

"I catechized my children through confirmation but we did not practice our faith as a family nor when the children grew up. Because of the impact Kendra had on me, her faith in God and the return to the Catholic Church, I finally decided to follow her lead."

Joan Berens, Kendra's Mother

"What I thought was the 'flavor of the month' transformed my wife and became a lifelong commitment to faith."

Jeff Von Esh, Kendra's Husband

AM I
CATHOLIC?

A Struggle with Faith, Humility, and Surrendering to God

KENDRA VON ESH

LEAD WITH COMPASSION

www.kendravonesh.com

A special thank you to my husband, Jeff, who married someone who is not who I am today and still loves me as much, if not more.

I adore you! Thank you for your never-ending support, direction, freedom, and guidance.

My loving mother, thank you for your inspiration and for being my best friend.

To my family and friends who have supported me throughout my journey, I love you all!

To all the people highlighted and referenced including my parishes and all forms of media, I wouldn't be where I am without you!

To everyone who has helped me with my professional transformation and to discover my voice. A special call out to, Jeff Baker, Sima Dahl and Angie Mroczka—your patience, hard work, and commitment continues to be remarkable.

From the Author

If you want others to be happy, practice compassion.
If you want to be happy, practice compassion.

–Dalai Lama

YOU ARE INVITED TO JOIN US IN

A group of spiritual souls aching for more joy, kindness, and empathy. Be inspired, motivated, heard, and most importantly—loved.

Each week I help you look through the lens of compassion showing you different ways to approach your life.

Visit www.kendravonesh.com/compassionate-culture to join.

Contents

Foreword

Last Sunday, March 4th, I attended Mass for the first time—ever.

I sent Kendra a picture from outside Christ the Redeemer Catholic Church before getting out of my car and making the somewhat hazardous trek across the parking lot and to the door of the chapel for the 5 pm service. She was cheering me on the entire time.

I sang the hymns, listened to the readings, and knelt in contemplation while everyone around me went to receive the Eucharist. When it was over, I left feeling lighter and, much to my surprise after kneeling so much, with none of the knee pain that plagues me on a daily basis.

If Kendra believed that she was the least likely person to find God, you would have seen me right in line with her. Growing up in a jumbled variety of different Protestant denominations, primarily

Southern Baptist, I grew up feeling no connection to my faith.

And, like Kendra, I tried to fill that gap in my soul with dozens of other substitutes—even going as far as to become Wiccan at one point.

But the truth is that none of those things gave me the sense of peace that I felt when I sat in that pew (not quite in the back row) and observed God at work in the hearts of the people around me that night.

And none of that would have been possible without this book, which I've read dozens of times while helping to bring it into this world. Whether it is your first time reading it or your fifteenth, you are in for a real treat.

Having worked very closely with Kendra for the last four months, she can only be described as a *force of nature*. I have observed how tirelessly she has worked to bring this book to life. She is a beacon of love and compassion—but most importantly, a reminder of hope for someone who believes that they are too far gone to deserve God's love.

If you are aching to return home, or are in the market for a new one like I am, He's ready and waiting to meet you right where you are.

—Angie Mroczka, 'Book Sherpa' and Author

Preface

In this book, I share my journey from a cradle Catholic, who learned *nothing* about what the Catholic Faith meant and lived in mortal sin, to a *devout Catholic* who attends daily Mass as often as possible and goes to confession at least twice a month.

Yes, a complete 180.

But the real hero of this story isn't me—it's you. You are why I've written this book, as an invitation to look inside and see if you too are coming up short on the pie chart that represents your life (more on that soon).

Jesus will meet you where you are—no matter what type of life you are leading and no matter if you are even searching for Him or not. I sure wasn't!

I want to help you understand Catholicism in the way my simple mind works, sharing the research I did into the Catholic Church as I sought out the truth. I also hope to show you how vibrant, peaceful, beautiful, and joyful your life can be with Jesus in it!

And I promise I am no holy roller so you won't get any of that 'holier than thou' stuff from me.

I purposefully kept this book short and light because who wants to read a heavy book on God if you aren't sold on Him yet and just looking in to 'things.'

I explain how I have aligned with the Catholic teachings, which was *not* the case at the beginning of my journey.

I felt compelled to write this NOW. Why?

Because I feel as if I am the least likely person to have found God, faith, or religion based on how I lived my life and how I chose not practice my faith for decades! Seriously, I am one of the biggest sinners I know!

But this is not a "tell-all" book. I am mortified at the things I have done in this life and the sins that I've repeated, over and over. I have confessed those to God through the Sacrament of Reconciliation, and thankfully, He has forgiven me. I battle all the time to live a better life and not to sin. It is a daily struggle.

I hope you find this book not only entertaining but enlightening and informative.

Ugh, I Need to Cleanse!

I have got to do something—I need to lose weight and get healthy!

Dr. Natasha Turner was on The Dr. Oz Show discussing a book she wrote called *The Hormone Diet*.

Basically, you cut out everything *except* organic, wild, free-range chicken, fish, and veggies. That meant no caffeine, no alcohol, no dairy, nothing in a package, no starchy carbs, and no beef or pork. It also included about 25 pills a day to detox your liver.

Then, after two months, you add back *one* food each week. The idea is to see if the foods cause a reaction or to see if you are allergic to something like wheat, dairy, etc.

Now, my husband Jeff has a major problem with me watching Dr. Oz.

Every new thing I see on his show is eventually bought or adopted in some way into our household. Don't get me started on all the workout DVDs I have in the house!

Let's just say Jeff was less than thrilled at my suggestion to go on this diet.

Now, why would we go through such a drastic change in our lives, you might ask?

In March of 2013, my dad had quadruple bypass surgery. There were NO warning signs that anything was wrong. It happened when he went in for some tests to see if he was ready for knee surgery.

Can you imagine?

"Hey, Doc, I want to have knee replacement surgery so I can golf," and after your test results they say, "Yeeeeaaaaah, not gonna happen, you're goin' in for quadruple bypass surgery at 7:00 am tomorrow!"

So, I figured I (meaning Jeff and me) needed to do something about the extra 15-20 pounds we were carrying because it could have easily been us my panicked mind thought.

I gotta love my husband; he deals with so many "flavors of the month" with me, he should be up for sainthood (at the time, I had no idea what a saint really was, by the way). Of course, there is a LOT more to do with sainthood than to put up with a whack-job wife like me, but it's a start!

As I began preparing the list for the groceries and the numerous supplements to purchase for the diet, I came across a pie chart in the book.

There was one piece of this chart that struck me hard because I hadn't even noticed it was missing. It said SPIRITUALITY, which I interpreted to be religion.

I am happy that I defined the word in that way because I may not have decided to go to church otherwise.

I reasoned that since I was cleansing my body, I might as well restore my soul and start going to church. So, I determined that I was going to do just that, knowing it would most likely result in me going solo.

I didn't really feel inspired about going to church; I think I was more pumped about starting the diet and losing weight.

I mean, can you blame me? Are *you* psyched to go to *church?* Not to mention, I was a bit nervous because I hadn't been in so long and clearly, I wasn't really a fan.

Now that I decided to add church to Easter Sunday, I was off to the grocery store!

Due to the divorces in our family, it is easier for us to get together for Easter *Saturday*. I usually host this holiday and this year was no exception. Everyone came over, and I proceeded to eat and drink everything in the house because the following day was the first day of the cleanse *and* my first day going to church—Easter Sunday!

Toward the end of the night, I shared my decision to go to church with everyone. I had picked out a "big box" church that was non-denominational and close to my house.

But it was my mom's boyfriend, John, who asked, "Why wouldn't you go to a Catholic Church?"

I didn't have a good answer after a couple of bottles of wine, and honestly, I wasn't sure. It was probably because I was living such an anti-Catholic lifestyle and I wasn't even sure I believed what the church taught. Would I be a hypocrite going to Mass?

But I was too buzzed to get into a deep conversation about it, so I fumbled with my smartphone and Googled the closest Catholic Church. I would go to Mass for my first Easter Sunday—done and done!

As for the diet, Jeff and I did it for a month, but we didn't feel much different. We didn't lose but a few pounds, and we still have half-full bottles of the craziest supplements in our cabinets even today—5-HTP anyone?

To my benefit, I have since weaned myself off Dr. Oz over the past few years. The one thing that is forever stuck in my psyche is flushing the toilet with the lid down.

He showed a demo of how much "stuff" goes into the air when you flush...

Let's just say, move your toothbrushes far from the toilet everyone!

2

Am I ... Uh ... *Catholic?*

Let me introduce myself.

I am the only daughter—a middle child in between two hockey-playing brothers.

If you know anything about hockey families, then you know they are invested and dedicated to the sport. My brothers happened to be very talented at the game, so there were many tournaments and time spent in ice rinks as I was growing up.

This meant, for me, that I had to find my own way and sports wasn't it. I was fortunate to have a lot of close friends in school and was a pom/pom and cheer leader through junior high and high school.

Even though I was a cheerleader and fairly likable, I thought, I was always negative and critical of myself. I was a bigger girl, which was one of the reasons I told myself I was on the squad. *Someone* had to be big enough to hold up the fliers, they needed a base!

I was always insecure and continuously compared myself, my family and life to others. I always wanted what I didn't have; including a lot of money to buy the stuff I *thought* I needed to make me happy.

I was blessed to have parents who paid for me to go to college, which was what kids just seemed to do back then. I had no real aspirations to be anything specific, but I knew I wanted to make a lot of money. Get the theme here?

I graduated from SIU Carbondale with a Communications/Public Relations major and double minor in Journalism and Psychology—Go Salukis!

Throughout college, I always compared myself to others but never measuring up. I was a good time, I was the partier, the first one to smoke, drink, and perhaps everything else. But I certainly had no clear direction on why I was at school or what I wanted to do as a profession.

After college, I started out in sales. I thought, with my personality, I could make a killing! But then there was this 'cold calling' thing, and I *hated* cold calling. I found out after a few years that I didn't have the best discipline to be a salesperson.

A friend told me about a position at a payroll company, ADP, where I supported clients with HR and payroll processing. I was recruited from there to a manufacturing company to implement SAP, which is an enterprise software system. That is where I launched my information technology (IT) career.

At 30, I was a Director of IT, at 37, I was a VP of IT, and at 40, I was a Chief Information Officer (CIO).

One of my goals was to achieve CIO status before I was 40 and when that came to fruition a few days before my 40th birthday, I was pretty darn proud of myself.

I did not have issues with money. I was not rich by any means, but I was comfortable and did not worry about anything financially. I was truly fortunate with my career, which took hold of me instead of *me* taking hold of *it*.

What do I mean by that?

I am NOT a technical person, and IT was not what I thought I would be "doing" for a living. See, I don't really have a *passion* for technology.

Sure, I like using technology and would die without my smartphone, but I was not super passionate about being an Operational Information Technology Executive. My career just happened *to* me.

At the time, I was okay with it because it paid well. It allowed me to do most anything I wanted—buy a house or two, a nice car, vacation, nice wine, eat out often, enjoy ALL the comforts this world had to offer.

So, what about my personal life?

I married my high school sweetheart at 26 and was divorced by 29.

We got married in the Catholic Church. I was keenly focused on my career, and he wanted to have kids. I went off the pill for a little while (yes, I was on the PILL) and then went back on the pill. We divorced soon after.

He is a wonderful man, was a great husband, and I am a better person for knowing him. Today, he is doing great with a wonderful wife and two beautiful kids. We still keep in touch, and I see him and his family quite often at my Goddaughter's events.

Did I mention he was pretty religious and his family was pretty Catholic? Even though we didn't practice going to church regularly, we did when we were with his parents.

Jeff, my second husband, has two amazing children/ young men who are in their early twenties with whom I adore.

Jeff and I moved in together in 2001, built a house in 2003, and finally got married in Mexico in 2006. I felt as if something was missing being married at a resort in Mexico and not in a church. Jeff, on the other hand, didn't much care but he wanted to make me happy. He said, "God is at the beach, too, ya know."

He supported my need to get married in a church, so a year later *to the day*, we were wed by a former co-worker who left his Corporate Communication job to become a pastor in a non-denominational ceremony. It was just the two of us.

As far as 'spirituality' is concerned, that piece of the pie wasn't entirely lacking—it was shaded in a bit for me.

The traditional definition of spirituality was something I possessed a bit; I had compassion for people, I loved animals and our earth. I believed in God, sometimes I prayed (mainly when I needed help, someone was ill, or when I was in a situation of some sort), and I truly felt there was a greater power than me. I would even seek out Christian radio stations when I was in the car on long trips because they made me feel good.

I had quite a few religious/spiritual conversations with people throughout the years as well. So, God did try to talk to me a few times; I just wasn't ready to listen.

As for organized religion, we were not practicing Catholics. Growing up, we went to public school and were chauffeured to CCD (Confraternity of Christian Doctrine) or religious education classes on the weekends.

I remember memorizing prayers in the back seat of the car in my soccer uniform just to "pass the test." We did not attend church regularly, but we were Chreasters (pronounced 'kreesters')—attending church every Christmas and Easter until early adulthood.

In my late twenties, I didn't go to church *at all*. I gave up something every Lent but never made it all the way through to the end.

I wasn't that sure as to WHY I was giving up something. I did not put together Jesus' passion, suffering, and death for all our sins to giving up and sacrificing 40 days before His death and resurrection.

And as for Advent, I was only interested in being the first one to get the chocolate out of the Advent calendar window for that day! I had no clue that it was a time to prepare for Jesus' birth.

Speaking of Jesus' birth, I was pretty sure He was just God's Son, I had no real understanding of the Holy Trinity—one God in three divine persons the Father, Son and Holy Spirit.

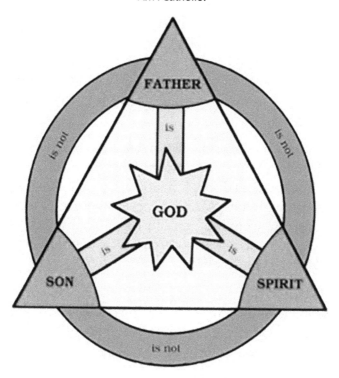

Image from Vatican Radio

I didn't identify myself with Atheists or other religions who did not believe in Jesus as Our Savior. Why? I am not sure, maybe blind faith?

Because surely, I didn't learn much from my religious education or any other religion for that matter to know the difference.

Yes, it is truly pathetic. How in the world was I able to get Confirmed? I knew almost nothing!

I do not think I am alone when I say that I did not learn what it TRULY means to be a Catholic. I only attended CCD, and when I was there, I was thinking of *anything* else, watching the time hoping it would somehow fly by faster than the clock would tick.

I didn't even learn the basics, but I am SO grateful my parents put me through the process. I was already marked through Baptism, Communion, and Confirmation as a Catholic, even though I wasn't quite sure what it all meant. I identified myself as a Catholic because my parents were Catholic, and they made me Catholic.

And now, all these years later, I was off to a Catholic Church even though I had some conflicts with the church's teachings and not sure the true meaning of the faith.

Some of the issues I had with Catholicism were:

- The priest sex scandals
- That birth control was not accepted (I didn't realize it was a Mortal Sin at the time)
- That gay "marriage" or same-sex attraction was not acceptable (what do I care who they love as long as they love each other?)
- It should be okay to get divorced (not really clear about the Annulment process)
- It should be a woman's decision to have an abortion (who am I to judge?)

And why not test the waters and live with the person before marrying them and avoid divorce altogether? Yes, this includes sex before marriage too (you want to test those waters as well). It all seemed logical to me so you can figure out if you are compatible or not.

So, what is my point sharing all of this with you?

I had a GREAT life, and I was thoroughly enjoying every second. I was drinking, laughing, and playing hard with great family and friends.

I was known as the party girl who said things that people only thought. I was the wild one, a truck-driving potty-mouth and the more I drank, the crazier I got.

Even though my job had its stresses and I was always worried about whether I was good enough—it paid well, so I stuck with it.

I was living the worldly life for sure. I never really thought that my moral compass was off, what my true meaning of being on this planet was, or religion, Heaven, Hell or eternity.

What in the world could I want other than the life I had!?!?

Well, I envied people who had more—bigger homes, better cars, more money, and possessions, people who had better bodies, more abilities, more drive, better education, more esteemed professions. It is no wonder why I made more people rich than myself trying every gimmick "as seen on TV" and all the "flavors of the month" concerning workouts, diets, get-rich-quick programs with real estate, and investments.

So, in my effort to fill in the "spiritual piece of pie" to complete my cleansing diet, I decided to go to the Catholic Church instead of the "big box" church.

This turned out to be a *pivotal* decision for me as it was the first step in my journey to the Catholic faith.

I thank God for putting John in my way that Easter Saturday evening when he said, "Why aren't you going to a Catholic Church?"

I also thank God for listening to my countless prayers the night before my Dad had his surgery. I believe that was all Jesus needed from me, to open my heart and to invite him in to take the wheel as we went down this scary road of heart surgery. My Dad's surgery was a success, and it was a quick recovery. Thank you, God!

And I also want to thank God for Google, which was more than helpful in my drunken stupor to find the nearest Catholic Church.

There are no coincidences—there are only "God-incidences."

3

And With Your Spirit?

Beep, beep, beep, beep...

"What the ... are you *kidding me*, it's time to get up already?" I rolled over to smack the snooze button. I was in FULL hangover mode.

Whose idea was this church thing anyway?

I crawled out of bed, scrounged up something church-worthy to wear, brushed my teeth, threw my hair up in a ponytail and out the door I went.

Clearly, I didn't give myself any time for grooming let alone reflecting. I allotted just enough time to get in the car, find a parking space close to the exit so I could get out before the traffic, get home and down some Tylenol before I crawled under the covers again.

It was a bit unnerving walking into this unknown church. I dipped my fingers in the holy water next to the door, and while I made the Sign of the Cross, I looked for a spot to sit.

Jackpot! I found one in the last pew at the end. YES—fist pump in the air!

The Mass was about to start because I saw Father Chris Kuhn walking down the aisle from the front of the church greeting people along his way. Then he turned at the last row toward the middle aisle of the church. As he passed by me and another man in my pew he sang, "Heeelllooooo, people in the back row." That made me smile and feel a bit more comfortable in this unfamiliar place. Seriously, any minute there could have been lightening striking me down!

He met up with the altar boys (they had girls, too) and prepared to walk down the aisle toward the altar.

The music started, and everyone had the Missal thingie in their hands singing. They stood up ... so I stood too.

Uh ... how do they know what page to sing from? I leaned over like a cheater trying to see the page number in the book of the woman in front of me. Arrr, to no avail, I could not see it!

Then we started Mass.

I must come clean here and tell you that I *never* followed along in the book before. Every time I went to church I just "followed" everyone else. Stand, sit, kneel, stand, kneel, sit and then in between trying to find an entertaining child or some horrible hairstyle or outfit that I could critique so I could pass the time as quickly as possible.

We started in the name of the Father, Son, and Holy Spirit. I passed that one! Woo Hoo!

Then Father Chris said, "Peace be with you."

At this point, I was feeling pretty proud of myself because I know THIS response ... "And also with...."

WAIT! They are NOT saying that!

What ARE they saying? When did this change and why wasn't I notified!?!?

I was pretty embarrassed because I sort of belted out my response, maybe the last word was soft when I realized they were saying something else.

Feeling like a complete idiot, I had to figure out this Missal thing. I checked out the lady's book in front of me again and was able to see the page number.

SCORE! I followed the Missal up until the Gospel.

Now, what was it they were doing on their forehead and chin (or was it lips) and chest when they said, "Glory to you O Lord?"

Hmmmmm ... I don't know.

And then I followed like a chimp—stood when they stood, sat when they sat, knelt when they knelt. I knew the Our Father and the Apostle's Creed (not the Nicene Creed, of course, that was way too long to memorize in the back of the car, and I wasn't tested on that one either).

Then it was time for Holy Communion. I panicked, breaking into a bit of a sweat. I drew a complete blank on what to say when I get up there!

Pa-the-tic!

I racked my brain the whole way up—it has to be "Amen" right? I tried SO hard to hear the person in front of me, but it was fruitless. So, I listened to my gut and said, "Amen" after the priest said, "The Body of Christ," and put the Host in my mouth.

He didn't laugh or drop his jaw, so I must have done it right!

Phew, back to the last row I went.

We were coming to the end of Mass. But first, the announcements.

Ugh, those dreaded announcements … will this ever end? They made mention of Divine Mercy Sunday the following week, and that confession would be held after Spanish Mass at 2:00. Interesting.

Wow, confession. I hadn't done that since I was about sixteen.

The last blessing *finally* came, the music began, and I darted toward the door before Father Chris could get down the steps to the front of the altar. "See ya!"

I skated out of there with NO traffic to contend with, and on my way back home, I was feeling pretty good about myself. That wasn't so bad.

During the week, I decided to Google the Mass and found out the response after saying, "Peace be with you" is now "and with your spirit," and that changed a few years prior. I also found out that I shouldn't have received Communion because I wasn't in a state of grace, that I condemned myself!

Ugh ... the Catholic Church, what is with all these *rules?*

How is one to know the right thing to do? Yeah, yeah, I know—they get catechized.

Looking back, I can say that I am *more* than amazed that I continued to go to church. And while I was regularly going, I began to notice things that had never caught my attention before.

What is INRI on top of the cross and what does it mean?

It means *Jesus the Nazarene, King of the Jews,* and was put there by Pontius Pilate. The high priest and Pharisees were not happy about that because they wanted it to read "Jesus SAID he was the King of the Jews," but Pontius Pilate bluntly stated, "What I have written, I have written." It was posted on the cross in three different languages.

Why do the priests wear different colored garments?

It starts with purple and ends with green, and there is a white and red in between.

What do the different colors used by the priest signify?

Different colors represent distinct parts of the liturgical/worship calendar or seasons. The primary colors have been purple, white, red, green, and black.

Purple is worn during Advent and Lent, representing the penitential (penance) sense of those seasons. Similar to purple is the color rose, which is worn just two Sundays during the year as a sign of hope and joy even during the more reflective/penitential seasons. First, is the Third Sunday of Advent, otherwise known as Gaudete Sunday. During Lent, it is worn during the Fourth Sunday, otherwise known as Laetare Sunday.

White denotes times of celebration as seen in the Christmas and Easter seasons. White vestments are also worn at Baptisms, Weddings, Ordinations, and feast days of the Lord, the Blessed Mother, and saints who are not martyrs.

Red implies the blood of Christ and the Holy Spirit. It is worn by the priest on Pentecost, Good Friday, for Confirmations, and for the feast days of martyrs.

Green signifies Ordinary Time in the church and the shade of the color green can vary. For instance, the green of spring is different than that of November as the church year ends. And I didn't even know there was a church year either.

I just thought it was this never-ending deal. Each liturgical year starts on the first Sunday of Advent and ends on the last Sunday of November.

Black, rarely seen, can be worn during the Office of the Dead. It may also be worn on Good Friday.

This is probably more than you would like to know and there are more articles and "garb" that I didn't share. I found it fascinating how much goes into their dress. Look it up, it is interesting, they show each piece and describe its purpose. It is interesting to me at least because it shows how the church is very deliberate throughout the season-specific to celebrations, penance, blood/martyrs and I didn't even know there were different colors for different purposes because I only went during Christmas and Easter = white.

There were other things I began to notice as I paid attention to Mass and I just kept looking things up as I went along. A lot of thought, ritual, tradition, and purpose goes into each Mass. I came to realize we go to *worship* God; it is not to be taken as an entertainment hour but serious time to prepare yourself to receive *the Lord* in Holy Communion and reliving His sacrifice for us and to deepen your relationship with Jesus. It is also fascinating to know that the Mass is followed the same across the world with a few regional nuances, but mainly the same. Everyone hears the same Gospel reading every Sunday. How incredible to think about the millions of people contemplating the same word of God at the same time!

I have a message to lay-people, you know, the ordinary folk who are *not* familiar with the practices and teachings of the Catholic Church.

Do NOT feel embarrassed for not knowing the rituals and traditions. My first experience was hilarious, and I was like a fish out of water. But I was there, I was putting forth the effort, and I was slowly but surely learning. It takes time, and you must know that your experience will be uniquely yours. I just want to say that Jesus meets you where you are, right at this time, I was slowly beginning to understand things as God wanted me to hear them. It was a long process for me, and He also gave me the gift of yearning for knowledge about Catholicism. I now have this unquenchable thirst to learn more and more. I am grateful he has given me this gift. The gift that is never fully given as I could never know it all.

I also have a message for priests and deacons. Please, do not assume everyone has read the Bible, knows the Gospel, the Mass or anything about the Catholic Faith. Assume everyone is "in the back row." Teach lovingly, explain, and educate in an entertaining way applying to our lives today as often as you can. I learn something new or hear something directly related to the situation I am living at that time at almost every Mass in the Scriptures or in the homily.

And may God bless you for your vocation, most importantly, for the Sacrament of Reconciliation (confession) and your countless hours of hearing our souls poured out to you for forgiveness! Thank you so much for your precious time.

4

Divine Blubbering Sunday

It was a beautiful Spring day in Chicago, so my husband and I decided to play golf.

As I mentioned earlier, I worried quite a lot about my job and I had *many* sleepless nights. I think I also began to grind my teeth and as a result, I had incredible neck pain. This day was no different. But I decided to "buck up" and golf anyway!

About halfway through the round, my neck pain was so severe that I thought I was going to cry. I told my husband I couldn't play anymore, that I needed to lay down and rest my head. Golfing was making it worse.

He understood and continued to play with the other two guys who were kind enough to give him a ride home afterward. Yay!

I got home, went straight up to bed with my two dogs and put my head on the pillow.

For some reason ("God-incidence") I was reminded that it was Divine Mercy Sunday. I checked the clock, and it was 1:00. I recalled that confession started after Spanish Mass at 2:00. I popped up and thought to myself, "I should go!" Who knows, maybe it will help my neck pain?

I began to recollect all the sins I committed since I last went to confession, which was 26 years ago! And there were MANY and some MORTAL!

I wrote them down on paper, almost filling both sides; then I jumped in the car and headed to church. I wish I knew about the "Examination of Conscience"—you should review and contemplate before your confession to be sure you are thorough. I just improvised.

When I arrived at the church I was amazed at all the cars, I had to park quite a few blocks away. When I opened the door, there were like a hundred people standing at the entrance the place was packed wall to wall! I learned they called the entrance area of the church the Narthex. The air was warm and stale since it was an 80-degree spring day. I looked at my watch and thought, "There is no freaking way this Mass is going to be over at 2:00!"

I sat outside on the steps and waited for what seemed like an eternity. I saw a priest walking to the church from across the street. I decided to stop him and ask if confession was still going to happen today. He said, "Yes, after this Mass is over."

So, I waited and waited. Finally, a few people trickled out of the front of the church, but most of them were congregating, talking and just hanging out. I found that quite interesting since I am the complete opposite, I cannot get out of there quickly enough! Perhaps it is the strong faith and family community of the Hispanic culture?

I made my way through the steamy church, and it dawned on me that I had NO CLUE where I was going! I was like a lost puppy, the only person walking around in a golf outfit not knowing where I was supposed to go for confession.

Low and behold, that same priest walked in the front of the church, so I went back to him and said, "Sorry to bother you again, but where do I go for confession?" He pointed to the green and red lights that were on the top of a hallway entrance. He said I should stand back there, by the wall and wait for the light to turn green.

So, I stood there, feeling terribly nervous. Would THIS be the priest who is going to listen to my confession? There goes my anonymity if it is! I felt my heart begin to beat harder and suddenly I did not want all the people to leave because then I would have to go in and actually do this!

The church started to empty out, and sure enough, the priest I talked to twice waltzed on by me into that hallway. He turned right into a doorway and then the magic green light came on. I began to slowly walk thinking … *this freaking guy knows who I am*!

I opened the door and was a bit shocked at what I saw.

It wasn't your typical confessional where you open a tiny door and go in a dark "box" of sorts, and the priest is on the other side of a screen. It was a pretty large room with a thick curtain that hung from the ceiling to the floor. Picture the thick curtains with the white plastic backing you found in cheap hotels back in the day, meaning 20 years ago.

I could see the priest's feet sticking out from under the curtain on his side. If I wanted to, I could just walk to the right and shake his hand. Of course, I stayed as *far* to the *left* as I could.

I walked up to this wobbly standalone kneeler with a wee bit of padding on it. I knelt and rested my elbows on the top ledge and pulled my paper out of my purse. I didn't want to show everyone in the church my double-sided confession, so I kept it hidden until now.

He greeted me, I am not sure what he said, but then I knew it was my turn. I started with, "Bless me, Father, for I have sinned … get a load of this … it has been about 26 years since my last confession!" I said this as if I was some sort of comedian and tried to make light of the fact that is has been a REAL long time.

He replied with a very sincere and soft, "Welcome back home."

Whoa…

I immediately lost it. I started crying, and I couldn't stop it! I could not see my words through the puddles of tears in my eyes which are now streaming down my face. I could barely get the words out, my throat hurt so bad trying to speak through the uncontrollable sobbing.

And I cannot believe I didn't bring ONE single piece of tissue in there with me, not ONE! The sleeve of my pullover took the brunt of the snots and tears.

We discussed my sins and then he then asked me to say the Act of Contrition. I froze. What? Uh, I have no clue what that is, I don't have that one memorized; if you recall it has been 26 years.

Naturally, he figured out, with the long pause, that I didn't know it. He said, "It is taped on the armrest on the kneeler if you need it."

Awesome! Brilliant! I read it aloud, and as I was reading it, I was really feeling the words.

And then he absolved me of my sins, which was the last signal for me to bawl uncontrollably *one more time*!

I cannot describe in words the feeling I had at that moment. It was as if I was "fainting" but still upright and coherent. I felt a bit like I was floating yet I remained on my knees. My whole body radiated with a sense of peace. Why in the world did I not go to confession a LONG time ago? That feeling was like the best drug I have ever had. (Uh, and I have had a few.)

He blessed me, and that was my signal to depart. When I got up to leave I made a *split-second* decision to walk around the curtain to hug the priest and thank him with all my heart.

What the heck, he knew it was me anyway! Why not thank the guy who just heard what seemed like a half hour of blubbering?

I asked him his name and if I could meet with him soon and he agreed. I turned to leave the room and tried to collect myself—there are people out there! I have no clue how long I was in there and felt a little self-conscious as I came out, thinking everyone waiting in line must have thought I was a murderer or something.

As I walked down the center aisle, I noticed the line and I was shocked that it was almost out the door! I was more than happy I was the first one there because I may have given up due to lack of patience and pure nervousness.

I was more than scared to go to confession but the way I felt when I left was more than worth it. You know the feeling when you don't want to work out, but when you do, you don't regret it and feel great? Well, multiply that by a gazillion, THAT is the feeling you have when you leave confession.

Let's not forget this is THE reason Jesus became a man. To die on the cross for ALL of our sins and to institute the Sacrament of Reconciliation to forgive our sins. This is integral to the Catholic Church's meaning and purpose.

This day will go down as one of the BEST days of my life! Another pivotal decision for me on my faith journey!

5

I Shouldn't Take Communion?

I was quite smitten with this Catholic thing and what I was feeling after a mere two weeks of going to church and the blessing of Divine Mercy Sunday triggering my confession.

I shared with my husband how awesome it felt. He nodded and said he was happy for me.

Of course, I said, "You should go, too!" He smiled, dismissed my comment immediately and went back to his regularly scheduled program. Surely, he thought that after two weeks I couldn't *possibly* be THAT into this religious thing. I am sure he thought this will be one of the "flavors of the month" that will go away soon enough.

I started to do some research on the church and stumbled across some pretty good articles, of which a fair portion I didn't understand. I had to look up all these fancy-dancy words used in the faith to make sense of it all. I think I read two sentences and had to look up *four* words!

Then God put a thirst in me for some Christian radio like I listened to when I was traveling in the car for work. I stumbled across Relevant Radio and listened to that a couple of times. I must admit, it drove me a bit nuts when I first heard it. My first impression was, "What the, who ARE these people? They are like those holy rollers that make me want to run in the other direction. Blech, can they possibly be THAT happy? Ugh ... they are sort of sickening."

But I gave it another chance and another chance. I kept listening because it seemed that when I tuned in, there were topics that were pointed *directly to me*. As if they knew *exactly* where I was and what I needed to hear *at that moment*. It actually freaked me out a little.

I would like to give infinite thanks to Reverend Francis J. Hoffman, Father "Rocky" who is the Executive Director and CEO of Relevant Radio and all of the Relevant Radio show hosts, producers, staff and phone operators. You have been instrumental in my faith journey and have saved my soul! I have learned so much and feel like I am part of the RR family and I strongly suggest you check it out and download the free app, too.

Now, I booked a meeting with the priest who heard my confession, so I could get more understanding of what I was doing and to start a dialogue versus me scouring the internet and radio. I was really interested in going to see him, but I wasn't sure what I was going there to talk about exactly. I told him my story, and we took it from there.

He gathered that I had no clue about the teachings of Catholicism. I told him I went to Easter Mass and received Communion (before I went to confession) and afterward I found out that was not appropriate. I also shared my marriages, the one in Mexico and the next year in a non-denominational church. He informed me that I needed to refrain from Holy Communion until we are Sacramentally Married in the Catholic Church.

WHAT?

Am I supposed to just sit there in church while everyone else goes up to receive the Lord? What will people think of me? What kind of sin did SHE commit? And more importantly, how do I get my husband to marry me for the THIRD time?

We discussed how important it was to be in a state of grace to receive Holy Communion and if I had committed a mortal sin or many venial sins, I should go to confession frequently. But even if I did go to confession, I could not receive Holy Communion because I was not Sacramentally Married in the Catholic Church.

C'mon, what is with all these rules? No wonder why people walk away from this religion!

At the end of our meeting, the priest gave me two books: *The Catechism of the Catholic Church* and *The Compendium—Catechism of the Catholic Church*. I felt bad that he didn't charge me for the books, so I donated on my way out. I lugged the books home.

And that was the last time I saw that priest, who was the school administrator, as he left that parish shortly after we met. And I have not met with another priest since. That is on my list along with reading the Catechism.

To this day, I have not broken the seal of either book. The Catechism is 900 plus pages, and the Compendium is a synthesis of the full Catechism around 200 pages. I have heard the Catechism referenced numerous times (mostly by Monsignor Swetland a host of a RR program) and I plan to eventually begin by reading the Compendium to further understand and speak knowledgeably about the Catholic Faith. I mean, it is what the entire faith is based on, it is on my list and should be checked off already.

Here is a little-known factoid. I was listening to John Harper's Morning Air program his guest was Monsignor Stuart Swetland. John mentioned that Monsignor Swetland, in 1992, was assigned to assist in researching and writing the Catechism in college. How interesting, Monsignor references the Catechism all the time on his show (Go Ask Your Father), which makes a lot of sense as he helped research and write it back in the day. Honestly, Monsignor Swetland is like Rainman recalling the Catechism off the top of his head, now I see why.

I believe I need a Spiritual Director to meet with regularly. I will explain more on this later, I am discerning my professional vocation, and I am struggling with it. Onto the list it goes.

That night, when my husband got home he barely stepped into the house, I blurted out, "We have to get married in the Catholic Church!"

He laughed and said, "Oh, three times a charm, huh?" And we left it at that.

6

I am en Fuego! (on Fire)

I was absolutely glowing. I was radiating this positive energy and people were noticing.

During this time things were very depressing and negative at work. Everywhere you turned, people were congregating in offices and complaining about the changes in our global company.

I found myself in constant "look at the bright side" mode with my team to keep them motivated. They would look at me strangely, I had a radiance about me, perhaps we could call it joy? It was noticeable to me and to everyone around me.

During those few weeks, my peers, my team, my family, and friends were all asking me, "What is up with you? You are radiating this energy. Are you on a new diet? Are you working out? Are you *pregnant*?"

I couldn't help but talk about my new-found faith, how fantastic I felt, and the unquenchable thirst I had for learning more about it. I still wasn't exactly sure why I considered myself a Catholic other than the fact that my parents were Catholic and raised me that way. Or what the differences were with Catholicism and other Christian faiths for that matter.

But I was starting to ask questions about why there were so many Christian faiths and why some were so hostile, especially to the Catholic Faith.

One of my peers at work was Protestant, and I asked him what the differences were between our religions. He looked at me with a very peculiar face, laughed and said, "We will talk about it one day, it will be a lengthy conversation."

We never did have that talk.

I called up the pastor who married Jeff and me to share where I was with Catholicism and my faith journey and asked him why he wasn't Catholic. He said, "I needed to be sure I could follow my faith. Did I believe in the Catholic Faith's teaching completely? Could I follow it? I decided I couldn't. It wasn't for me."

That gave me pause. I was weeks into this, and I was learning that there were many rules in the Catholic Religion, and quite a few of these rules *I wasn't sure I agreed with either.* I continued to listen to the radio and researched things I had heard on the programs or at Mass. With some things, God gave me ears to hear. Other stuff I wouldn't understand for a few years. I saw the light in some areas, but it was still pretty dark in others.

During this time, we were living in our winter home, and I was attending Mass there. We were getting ready to pack up our belongings and move to our lake house for the next six months.

I had to find a church to go to near Fox Lake because I knew I wouldn't drive an hour back to the church by our winter home.

I mapped the closest one to the lake house because I am NOT a morning person or frankly a night person either. I *love* my sleep and will take as much of it as I can.

First, I picked a church down the street.

When I arrived at Mass, there were three people on one side of the door and three people on the other side of the door. They were holding the Missal books and welcomed me with what I should have accepted as a loving and welcoming greeting, but it struck me as invasive to some degree, almost creepy. The best way I can explain it is that I wanted to be by myself at Mass. I tried to sit in the back pew alone, far away from people so I could get the most out of Mass. I didn't want people to try to get me to volunteer or something if I got to know them. I know, right, how Christian of me?

I was also uncomfortable when I shook people's hands when we said, "peace be with you." And I was also quite miffed when some people would plop down next to me or right in front of me when there were MANY other places for them to sit. Hellloooo, can you give me some space, please?

I wasn't particularly fond of the style of the inside of this church. It had a wooden ceiling with beams across the top and a simple altar. A simple cross and some basic stained-glass windows that a child could have made with that colored sprinkled plastic in a cookie cutter mold baked in an oven. Sorry, I am just honest.

Where is the *beauty* of the old churches with the timeless décor, sculptures, art and the spectacular old-world style that takes your breath away when you walk inside? I decided that I needed to find another place to go to Mass, this one just wasn't for me.

I found my next parish, St. John the Baptist Church, in Johnsburg. It looked like the church I grew up in, it had that old-world church feeling to it. When I walked in, I felt a sense of peace, and it felt like home. Even though this was an extra ten minutes from my house, I determined *this* was the parish for me. I believe I felt the Holy Spirit giving me the "thumb's up" and *we* found our church at the lake.

A quick story—my mother and father-in-law have a hobby of going to garage and estate sales then they resell what they buy (after a bit of work) at an antique show. My mother-in-law has been doing this as long as I have known her. They restore or refurbish something that they bought for $10 and sell it for something close to 10-50 times that amount. Or they find something of great value that the seller has no clue about—it is a pretty unique talent they have.

My husband used to call it "junking" and sometimes we went along with them. I would putz around and pick up anything that looked old or rusty and say, "Is this worth anything?" Clearly, I had no clue.

This meant we did a lot of driving around. One day we pulled into a parking lot to turn around, and my father-in-law said, "Wow, look at this beautiful church. What kind is it?"

I looked at the sign and said, "It's a Baptist church, let's get moving along."

Guess what, it was THIS church ... St. John the Baptist Church.

We still laugh at that to this day! Yes, this was before my faith journey began. Can you say, "Clueless Catholic?" I can!

Sunday came and I, of course, started in the back row of St. John's. There was quick and easy access to the parking lot, meaning I could bust out of there before the traffic, you know the drill.

The pastor was a man from Poland with a cute accent that took me a little while to understand and get used to, Father Jacek Junak. There was also another priest who was a younger gentleman. When he preached his homily for the first time, I was shocked. He stuttered. Who would put a priest up there who stutters?

Looking back, I was *so* judgmental then. What a wicked person I was! I grew very fond of him, *and* his stuttering as my faith and compassion for people grew. I have learned that every single one of us is carrying our own crosses and we *all* have our own problems and issues. Every ... single ... one ... of ... us. But I didn't view the world like that at the time, only the past few years.

Then after a few short months, he announced that he was moving on to another parish. I sat in my pew and cried. I was really going to miss him.

After a couple weeks, I started trying out different parts of the church. In the back on the left, in the back on the right, then I spied a side door to a side walkway to the parking lot.

BINGO! I found an even FASTER way to my car! So, I started to sit there. It was there I met this woman who introduced herself to me after Mass since we sat close to each other. Oh no! I don't want to meet people. I was there only for myself. She was so nice, and it was good to see her when it was time to give peace.

Then I met another guy, and we ended up talking on the way out to the parking lot as he was right behind me most every Mass leaving before the end of the closing hymn, too. He also had a lake house.

Soon enough, I met most of the people around the same section where I sat or at least we were all familiar with each other. It felt good to sit around these people every Sunday at 7:00 and it made giving peace more comfortable for me. And then I moved from the last row to the front row. I was really getting into Mass, so I wanted to be closer to the action!

Later that summer, we had a party and my cousin, who lives in Johnsburg, came over. It seems as if I cannot go anywhere or speak to anyone without my faith coming into the conversation eventually.

I recall telling my cousin that I was going to Mass regularly and she looked at me in shock and exclaimed, "Why?"

If you could have seen her face, it was as if she was saying, "WTF are you doing *that* for?" in a tone as if to question my sanity.

Ironically enough, when I told her where I was going, she said, "Oh, we got married at St. John's." I could only connect the dots, another Catholic who has fallen away or was not truly catechized. At the time, I didn't quite see this pattern with many Catholics, but I do now.

The summer flew by. God was still knocking, and I kept opening my heart. I began to truly understand what Mass was about and I looked forward to going every Sunday. I still remained on my knees not able to receive Holy Communion as I was not married in the Catholic Church.

The Holy Spirit was working hot and heavy inside me—I was very into learning about Catholicism. I have *never* in my life found something that I enjoyed learning so much about. Nothing! You would have to PAY me to go back to school. I hated school! I was only there for the social part of it, and my grades were mediocre at best. I hated studying, and math was my nemesis. I remember crying at the kitchen table many a night with my Dad who tried to teach me basic math. I just hated it.

So, I find it bizarre that now I was learning and yearning to learn every day about *Catholicism*. WHAT? Hours and hours listening, online, reading. Crazy I tell you, *nobody* is more amazed than *I* am! God's grace is in me, I can feel it.

I think that I am the least likely person to have found God, purely because of who I am and how I lived my life which was pretty much anti-Catholic. I believe that is why my faith comes up so much with people. I am shocked about my faith, I wasn't looking for God, he found me where I was. I think everyone, including myself, is quite shocked by this new way of living and looking at life, through the lens of God, unconditional love.

I approached Jeff again about him marrying me in the Catholic Church. He said, with a bit of an annoyed tone, "Honey, I have NO desire to do that. I know this is great for you, but it is not for me. Can we please drop this?"

Hmph. Well, that didn't go so well. I was pretty much shut down with no further conversation. At that moment, all I could do was say, "Ooookaaay." I was a silent, disappointed pouter for the rest of night.

As summer ended and October came, we moved back to our winter home. I decided to go to confession at another parish, which was a bit closer than the one in Elgin because they had times that worked better for me. Oddly enough, both are named St. Mary's.

This one is in Huntley, and you should see the size of this place! The line for confession on a Saturday morning was ridiculous. They had three priests to keep things moving. I still don't get why people think confession is a bad thing; good, practicing Catholics go ALL THE TIME. Stop being scared and GO ALREADY! The sense of peace and relief you feel is far greater than any fear you go in with, trust me on that!

As I walked through this massive establishment, I noticed they had a 24-hour Eucharistic Adoration Chapel. I heard about this on Relevant Radio. Eucharistic Adoration is where you are in the presence of Jesus in the Eucharist.

What is the Eucharist, you ask?

It means "Thanksgiving" and is the official name of the Host/Communion 'wafer' that is consecrated to the Body and Blood, Soul and Divinity of Jesus during Mass. It is displayed beautifully in a monstrance on the altar in the church or in a chapel.

Yep, you bet I had to look up what the Eucharist was displayed in, I had no clue! A "Monstrance" is the vessel used in the church to show the consecrated Eucharistic Host, during Eucharistic Adoration. It is like a beautiful gold sun with rays holding the Eucharist right in the middle, so now *you* know!

Bottom line, you can sit with the Lord outside of Mass in complete silence, praying, reading and talking to God. How cool is that?

If you believe that the Eucharist IS the Body and Blood, Soul and Divinity of Christ, which is a fundamental belief of the Catholic Church, this is the single most generous gift to us Catholics ever! The Eucharist is the source and summit of our faith. And having the ability to sit with Jesus 24 hours a day, seven days a week is a gift beyond words.

Adoration soon became a place where I frequently visited during some pretty big trials over the next few years. It pained me when we would move back to the house in Fox Lake. I yearned for a church that had Perpetual Adoration 24/7 to spend time in the presence of the Lord when it was convenient for my busy schedule.

We went back to the lake to spend a weekend, and I went to confession at St. Peter's in Antioch on Saturday morning. A gentleman and I were the only two there, and the confessionals were fairly old that we could hear almost every word the man was saying inside.

It was a bit uncomfortable for us to sit there and listen to what we should not be hearing. The man in line with me knocked on the door and said, "Excuse me, we can hear you ... you might want to lower your voice." That didn't seem to work, so we struck up a conversation instead of standing there listening to him.

I told him St. Peter's wasn't my regular church, but I drove up there because of confession Saturday morning.

I shared with him that I missed the 24-hour Eucharistic Adoration Chapel at my other parish. Then he shared a gem with me. Marytown— National Shrine of St. Maximilian Kolbe, which was about 30-40 minutes away in Libertyville. It is a gorgeous shrine and has Perpetual Adoration.

I had never been to a shrine before, it was absolutely *stunning*. One of the items on my list is the walking tour and the Heavenly walk on the property. When I visited the first time, I stopped at the gift shop and lost an hour walking around in there! Before I left, I dropped almost $200!

Now, let's go back to St. Mary's in Huntley. After I discovered the Adoration Chapel and began to leave the church, I saw a display case of CDs. I meandered over to check it out. The titles looked cool, I picked up *Jesus Is...* by Father Michael Schmitz and a few more.

I dropped my money in the slot and off I went. My secular mind thought, "Hmmm, that is pretty trusting having the CDs available for anyone to take and expecting them to pay the amount they ask for without anyone 'manning' it." I always give more than what they asked for, just sayin'.

I was excited to have these in my car to help me on my quest on why Catholicism and its teachings. I soon became an addict of these CDs, and I didn't have anywhere to put them anymore. My glove compartment, center console, side door storage soon became full, and I started to fill my passenger's seat.

I devoured many CDs, and I learned so much about Catholicism and why people are Catholic or converted to Catholicism. My husband teases me to this day that I have no idea what is going on in the world because all I do is listen to Catholic radio and my CDs. I laugh because it is so true!

One of my favs is Matthew Kelly. He is very down to earth and pretty funny. His CDs turned me onto a few of his books.

In his book, *Rediscovering Catholicism*, he asks the reader what are you going to say when you are face-to-face with God, and he asks you, "So, what did you think of my book?"

I was dumbfounded. I have never read the Bible. Sure, I hear Gospel readings during Mass (and heard someone reading some words but I wasn't listening for the past 42 years), but I *never* picked up a Bible and actually *read* it.

We didn't have one in the house, and I do not think I have even seen one where I could touch it with my own hands. I have always thought it was a bunch of thee's and thou's and blah, blah, blah mumbo jumbo. I thought I would want to poke my eyes out if I ever read it that is if I stayed awake long enough to get through a few chapters. I didn't own a Bible, I wasn't sure if there was a Catholic version vs. other versions. I surely wasn't educated on the fact that some Christian Bibles have some books actually removed from theirs.

So, what *would* I say to the Lord? "Uh, sorry, I just thought it would be too boring! You got a Cliff's Notes version or something I can watch on TV?"

But then I found the next best thing since sliced bread, the Internet, and smartphones and I heard about it on Relevant Radio. You can download The Truth and the Life Dramatized AUDIO BIBLE!!!

Whaaaaaaat?

Yep, you heard me! The entire New Testament can be played like a movie in your ears with characters and sound effects. It is absolutely fabulous, and it downloads to your smartphone so you can listen all the time, you do *not* need to be online!

Plus, you can immediately go to any book, chapter and verse quickly with a few touches of your finger and it is right on your phone! No more carrying around another book. It also has definitions of some phrases and references to the Old Testament. You can flag parts of the Bible, add notes, etc.

I did end up buying a brand-new paper Bible when I was at Marytown, part of the $200 shopping spree. I figured I *should* have one and this one had maps and other color pictures to educate me as I thumbed through it. A Bible with pictures, cool, I am showing my immaturity here I am sure! It remains in my drawer, un-opened like the Catechism, but it is *in my house* and on my ever-growing list of things to read.

I have had a few movies impact me like no book or CD ever will.

The first one I was exposed to was "The Exorcist." I remember that movie, distinctly. I only saw it twice, and I don't ever want to see it again.

I think I was about ten or eleven when my brothers and I decided to watch "The Exorcist" while my parents went out for the night. We were all in our pajamas, one brother is two years older than I, and the other is six years younger.

We started the movie and somewhere when it got super scary, we all laid on top of each other. Picture us all on the couch. My older brother on his stomach lying on the bottom, I am on his back on my stomach, and my younger brother was on my back. We were so freaking scared, and I am pretty sure we weren't supposed to watch it, but we did.

I had nightmares for months. I would bet my life that both of my brothers recall that night and us laying on each other. I am sure they had bad dreams, too!

Then when I was 30, a girlfriend of mine had never seen the movie and was curious because it was recently released in the theaters. I told her I would go with her.

I watched the whole thing through the spaces of my fingers. It was quite a different experience on the big screen. I had a sick-to-my-stomach feeling throughout the movie. We were both so scared that we decided we would talk to each other the whole way home, both of us were living solo at that time, to be sure we got in the house safe and sound. And the nightmares started up again.

I don't get the vampire or those crazy shows that are out there today where they are demon-like, from the underworld, zombies, etc. I have never been a horror film person either. Give me an action film, romantic comedy or animated movie any day over horror and gore.

"Friday the 13th" was another one that stayed with me for a while, and that darned "Halloween" movie music is chilling. Deee de de de....de...de...de... de—you know the tune. "The Omen" was another one that made me sick. I was staying overnight at a friend's house and a bunch of us watched it. I felt so sick to my stomach that I had to call my mom to pick me up. And lastly, the movie "Magic" just about scared me away from puppets forever!

Now let me share some movies that impacted my life more positively.

My mom asked me to go see "Terms of Endearment" with her when I was about thirteen years old. Keep in mind, my mom and I didn't really do much stuff together as mother and daughter when I was younger. I remember that movie like it was yesterday and I recalled crying like a baby and realizing how complicated and special a mother and daughter relationship can be. And, of course, losing a loved one makes you think about your own mortality.

In 2014, she asked me to go see "Heaven is for Real." I remember hearing about it on Relevant Radio, but I think she heard it from her church (yes, I said HER CHURCH—stay tuned for more with my mom). I knew I wouldn't get Jeff to go and thought it would be great to see it with her. She did giggle at me crying during it! And the funny thing is she cries just about as much as I do. You should hear us sometimes on the phone, either one of us can get the other started—it's hilarious.

Way back in 2006, I saw "The Passion of The Christ" on TV by myself, and it was gripping. This was before my faith journey began. I remember being horrified by the brutality and yes, I cried a

LOT. Talk about a sick-to-your-stomach feeling, it was so brutal the scourging and the Crucifixion.

I believe this was God igniting something in me.

One thing to add to my list is to watch "The Case for Christ" with my husband and boys. I asked my husband if he would give that to me for a gift and one day he said, "Yes." Then when I wanted to watch it, he was not at all interested. Can you say, "denied?"

I am going to ask all three of them to watch it with me for my birthday this year, only a month away, they better watch out!

Speaking of my birthday...

7

Best Birthday Ever!

This will be a very short chapter, but it was such an extraordinary day for me that I wanted to call it out.

As we were getting settled in our winter home, October cruised on by. It is always a crazy month for us.

When my birthday arrived in November, I didn't expect a gift.

Sometimes we buy each other birthday gifts, many times we don't. Sometimes we remember our anniversary, sometimes we don't—and neither of us gets upset about that.

We do not buy Christmas or Valentine's day gifts either. The way we think of it is if we want something, we'll buy it. No need for a special day to do that. Some other couples we know think that is a bit bizarre, but it works for us.

That night, I was sitting at the kitchen island with a glass of wine. Jeff was a little later than usual, so I figured I would help myself to some cheer since it WAS my birthday. But I never needed a special occasion to have some wine.

Jeff came in with a small box.

I can't recall if he had flowers or not. All I thought of was, "Oooooo, a small box, you know what they say, 'Good things come in small packages,'" so I assumed it was some beautiful jewelry.

After I tore off the wrapping and lifted up the cardboard lid, I pulled out the velvet box.

Was it another wedding band?

Quick story. I tossed my wedding band into the Salvation Army Red Kettle one day coming out of the grocery store.

I had no dollars, so I grabbed all the change in my wallet. The back of my wedding ring looked like a nickel, the other side of my wedding band was filled with one carat of diamonds. I never saw anything on the news about the ring and sincerely hope that the $1,000 value was actually donated!

But I digress.

Maybe it is a pair of diamond stud earrings? I had been eying some a while back.

After saying, "Ooooo, what could this be?" I flipped the lid open, and I was speechless at what I saw.

It was a Cross on a necklace.

A simple silver Cross on a thin silver chain. No bling, no diamonds, nothing flashy. And it was the most beautiful thing I had ever seen!

I immediately started bawling—my eyes filled with tears so fast, I couldn't contain myself. I looked up at Jeff and saw that HE was crying. I am not sure what he expected from me as far as a reaction, but this was the best gift I have ever received from him.

Not even my wedding ring could compare!

I was so touched. I said something along the lines of "so what made you get this for me, this is so perfect? I adore it and love you so much!"

He said something about being amazed by the faith I had and admitted he had expected it to be another "flavor of the month." He was truly proud of my commitment.

I did not take the opportunity to bring up the fact that I still wanted to get married in the Catholic Church, the moment was *too* spectacular.

I love my husband so much. I pray every day to all the angels, saints (St. Monica specifically), Jesus, Mary, my Guardian Angel, his Guardian Angel, Joseph, Holy Spirit, and ANYONE who can hear me for his conversion. He has gone to church with me for Christmas once or twice and during a regular Sunday Mass, but that was about it.

I have realized that I cannot be the Holy Spirit and convert him. All I can do is be persistent in prayer for his conversion (and my family and friends as well) and try every day to be a better witness of my faith.

8

I Yearn for the Eucharist

As November flew by, we approached December.

I learned, for the first time, that Advent is the preparation for the birth of our Lord Jesus and NOT about the chocolate in the windows of the Advent calendar when I was a youngster. Go figure!

I think the windows said something about the preparation of our Lord coming and each day had a different message. But I didn't care, I just wanted the chocolate. No wonder why I struggled with my weight!

I decided that this particular year, I wanted to participate in Advent and to deepen my prayer life. I bought Advent candles and tried to light them each week at dinner and say grace. I suck at remembering grace, add that to the list!

Before, I never paid any attention to the pink and purple colors during Advent because I was only at church on Christmas! I did not even notice the wreath up there on the altar either. I now look forward to this time as it gives me pause to reflect and make sacrifices for our Lord and celebrate His upcoming birth.

Advent and Christmas came and went quickly, as they always do.

I did my best to light the candles and try to prepare for the Lord's coming, but it wasn't the best attempt if I am honest. I didn't slow down like I should have, and I didn't spend more time in silence, I let the secular shopping flurry take hold of the season instead of Christ, who IS the season. And poof, it was gone in a flash.

The new year arrived and what was my resolution going to be? To lose weight; again, for the umpteenth time!

As always, I started off the year "all in" eating healthy, working out, not drinking, only to go off the wagon a few weeks later.

Then came Lent.

I have always given up things at Lent, it was one thing I learned, but I did not know the TRUE meaning of *why*. Honestly, I would give up things like sweets, chocolate, wine, fattening foods for the real reason … wait for it … wait for it … to lose weight!

It was all about *me*. I didn't give anything up to show the Lord that I could make sacrifices for

Him as He did for us when He gave up His life in a humiliating fashion, hung on a Cross for all the world to mock him, naked, in the most horrific form of capital punishment. Nope, I did it for me and my shallow worldly focus on me, myself and I.

This year we decided to give up alcohol, which was a huge deal for us. Our way to pass the time and end our stressful day is usually with some wine and Jack and Diet Coke which is Jeff's poison.

You should have seen us rationalizing it from the very beginning. First, it was giving up alcohol completely. Then we changed it to "during the weekdays" then we went on vacation and said, "Well, we must drink on vacation so we can tack on a few days after Easter."

Then we had a party and then another event, and soon we had tacked on three weeks to abstain after Easter. Although we did quit drinking periodically through Lent, we never followed through on our additional three weeks.

Do you remember when I said God gave me ears to hear *early* in my faith journey and ears to hear other things much *later*? This was one of those times when I could have used a big Q-Tip to clean out the wax!

I really didn't connect the sacrifice I was doing with the sacrifice that Jesus did for us and for our salvation. In plain words, Jesus took ALL of humanity's sins with Him on the cross and died for us. He set up the best sacrament known to all of us sinners on the planet—Reconciliation (confession). What a gift, having our sins absolved by a priest and starting over, after penance—again, hoping and committing to do better every day and when we fall, try to be better again.

Now, when I approach Lent, there is no, "we can add days, we can tweak this, we can do that."

I now know my sacrifice shows my love and gratitude for Him, that what I am giving up is probably not good for me anyway and is a selfish and worldly desire. I need to show some self-mastery in my life.

I am also considering not giving up sweets or alcohol but giving up my precious "me time."

One of the things I do not do is volunteer my time. I am generous financially, but I also have the gift of time I can donate. I am selfish that way, I still do not volunteer, and I wonder why not?

Well, I'll tell you why not.

Because I travel a lot for my job and I am away from Jeff many nights, when the weekends and evenings at home come, I want to spend my time with him. I could do it, but I choose not to, I choose me and Jeff.

This is another thing that I need to add to my list. I feel I can make a difference. My mom and I have talked about it recently, but we have done nothing—pure laziness and selfishness.

Now, I have *still* not received the Eucharist at Mass, and I started to become resentful toward Jeff. I have had a bit of a 'tude' with him over the past few months, and I am beside myself wondering if I will ever be able to receive the Lord.

I know this is the purpose of the Mass and I cannot believe I cannot partake!

It was a pleasant evening, and we were sitting outside. I looked at Jeff and told him how my heart ached to have the Eucharist, what it means to Catholicism, and that I was starting to resent him for keeping me from receiving the Lord. Every week was a reminder of his decision to shut me down and not marry me in the Catholic Church.

I wonder if I did the right thing by saying it in that way. I felt like I forced him to agree to marry me so that I wouldn't be upset with him. Well, let's face it, I kinda did.

He agreed to marry me. The last thing he wanted to do was cause me that pain and put stress on our relationship.

I was elated, frankly. I really didn't care if I *encouraged* Jeff. We *should* be married in the Catholic Church anyway. Especially now with my new-found faith!

John 6:53

> "Unless you eat my flesh and drink my blood you shall have no life in you."

I began to make calls and made an appointment with Father Chris Kuhn (the one who said, "Heeeelllooooo, people in the back row" at my first Easter Sunday Mass).

Jeff was an amazing man throughout the process. And it WAS a process. Again, can the Catholic Church make things more difficult or put up more hoops for people to jump through? Apparently, they can!

Jeff was raised Catholic like me but didn't learn much, like me. He was previously married, but he was married in the Lutheran church so his marriage "didn't count" if you will (or follow form). So, he didn't have to do much of anything, which was a *relief.* We just needed to get his Baptismal certificate, wedding certificate, divorce decree and he was good to go.

My ex-husband filed an Annulment very quickly after we were divorced so if/when he ever fell in love again, he could marry in the Catholic Church. The good thing was that he had the Annulment granted and I signed the papers a few years prior, so we were all set, too.

It took quite some time to get it back from the Vatican so if anyone is looking to file an Annulment, just know it is a long process and can take months or years, so you might want to get on that.

Now I needed to get my stuff together. I called my mom and asked her where I was Baptized. The sad and funny thing is she didn't know! She gave me a couple parishes. I called the one, and they had no record. Then she gave me another parish and luckily, they had it.

At the time I did not know that I was talking to Father Richard Simon from "Father Simon Says" on Relevant Radio. He was just starting his radio program. He is the priest at St. Lambert's Church in Skokie where I was Baptized, and he was very helpful. I have grown very fond of Fr. Richard Simon's show. I was just listening to him this past week, and he said, "If you know an Atheist get him or her to watch the movie 'The Case for Christ!'" I mentioned earlier that I asked my two boys and husband to watch it with me for my birthday gift.

This is an example of the many things I hear on the radio that hit me and my circumstances at that moment. I don't think either of my boys or husband are Atheists, but it goes to show if he is recommending the movie to people who do not believe in Jesus or a God then it should prove to be a doozy for those three!

Now, back to the lack of my religious upbringing, clearly, we were NOT practicing Catholics whatsoever and "the thing to do" was to catechize your children, so my parents went through the process, whether I learned anything or not. I just find it funny you don't know where your child was Baptized. I have to say, I am SO grateful to them for still going through the process!

I wonder if any of this would have happened if I wasn't already a Catholic. Would I have done my research on the Catholic Faith and still came to the conclusion that it is the full truth? Would I go through the RCIA program (Rite of Christian Initiation of Adults), which is where adults go to become Catholic? I think it is a couple year process. I am not so sure I would do that, or would I? So, when I tease my mom about not knowing where I was Baptized, *I don't care*, I am just happy that I *was*!

The next step was Pre-Cana. This is a requirement for the bride and groom to attend before they get married. It is a day-long event ensuring the couple is prepared for all that marriage entails and to confirm they will live according to the faith. We drove an hour north on a beautiful Saturday to St. Bridget in Loves Park for the entire day including dinner, Mass *and* the opportunity to go to confession.

Jeff was a real trooper. He didn't complain at all.

The only part we were not really digging was the Natural Family Planning part of the day. This might gross you out, but I think it's funny. We still laugh at the cervical mucus method, where you put your finger inside your vagina and then touch it to your thumb to see if you have this thick stringy mucus. Eeeeeewwwwww. When the mucus is present, voila, you are fertile and can make a baby! We still joke about "mucus" to this day! Hey, it's a physical fact of hormones, might sound gross, but we found it pretty funny and leave it to me to share.

I was still on the pill then. I would find out that being on the pill is also considered a MORTAL SIN!!!

Are you kidding me? You mean I will go straight to Hell, no collecting $200, no 'get out of Hell free' card? Again, Catholic Church, you're killing me here with your rules!

While we were there, I tried to convince Jeff to go to confession. He pretty much shut me down like he did the first time I asked him to get married in the Catholic Church. Using almost the same language and tone, "I have no desire to do that."

Even after I told him he could not receive Holy Communion with me at our wedding. It didn't matter to him, and he didn't go to confession. I, on the other hand, didn't need to go to confession because I was regularly going anyway, and I decided to sit with him while other people confessed, and we closed out the evening with a Mass and a certificate. They have to wait until the very end, so you don't sneak out early to give you the certificate.

Pre-Cana—DONE—check!

Now we are at the final meeting with Father Chris, we went through all the documentation and the last part of our session he asked if we went into this marriage willingly and *if we were both open to having children* before we signed the papers.

What?

I don't remember being asked that the first time I got married in the Catholic Church. Uh, I am ashamed to say, Jeff and I lied to Father Chris. I couldn't WAIT to go to confession after doing that, and I did it at another church because I thought Father Chris would recognize my voice!

Then I started hearing a lot of stuff on the radio about the pill, how it was different from Natural Family Planning. I thought NFP was just another form of birth control but learned that it was very different.

There is much more to this that I won't go into in this book. And it did take a while for me to "get it." I will have a blog on this on my website as it is a pretty intricate thought process and took me a while to understand what the difference was between NFP and the pill and why one was acceptable and one wasn't.

www.kendravonesh.com/pill-vs-nfp/

The fact that birth control was a mortal sin certainly got my attention. Now I needed to get off the pill. How was THAT going to fly with Jeff?

I went off the pill a few months later, but only after Jeff got a vasectomy. Now, that is not any different than birth control, much more permanent and he is mutilating his body, I know. But Jeff was not willing to take a chance and honestly, neither was I, on having a child so late in life. I was mid-40's and Jeff early 50's.

So, this was a bit "bass-akwards" justification.

Funny how we can rationalize things in our feeble human minds. We made this fit in with our morality, and I did confess that I pushed Jeff into a vasectomy because I was definitely going off birth control. He was very reluctant to have a vasectomy (also a mortal sin). But I told him that I could not stay on the pill any longer knowing it was a mortal sin and because I had been on it for decades it is a carcinogen for crying out loud! So, bottom line, I am going off the pill. Now, what are you going to do? Oh, by the way, here is a place that does laser procedures so no cutting, no frozen peas, lickety-split.

Let me be clear, neither of us did the right thing! We should have trusted in God and NFP, and if it were His will, we would have had a child. If not, we wouldn't.

But I wasn't quite there yet ... to trust God *that* much... just being honest with you. I can and *should* control this ... I don't need to trust in *God*. What a fool I was!

I regret taking the pill and exterminating so many possible lives. I wonder what my life would have been like if I had been open to life. I am more than blessed that our two boys, now young men, have been in our lives for so many years. At least I was able to experience them as children helping to influence them to be loving, self-sufficient young men. I am so proud of who they have become.

But what I will never know is a life growing inside of me, relying fully on me to take care of the precious life bestowed on you and your spouse. How much of a bond that would be with your spouse, to create a life together, to watch each other appear in the new life you made in the love of each other.

Wow.

But God knew that the world couldn't take another ME! Laughing out loud over here, people who know me are laughing, too.

It just wasn't in God's plan for me as he didn't give me a "pill baby" either. You know, the small percentage of women who get pregnant while on the pill. I will always wonder what our lives would have been like if we had a child together.

Speaking of life ...

9

Thank You for Saving My Life

My mother is wonderful.

She is the most non-judgmental person I know. I tell her everything, I am so blessed that she is in my life. Anytime I need her, she is there, she is so honest and loving with me, and has been following me on my faith journey.

We were talking about the wedding, and I asked her what day would work best for her and John so we could ensure they were there because we need at least two witnesses. She mentioned that May 1st was her mother's birthday and it would be great if we could have it on that day, to make it even more meaningful.

Turned out it was a Thursday, and we could have the wedding that evening.

Done! Thursday, May 1, 2014, it was!

Thursday has a special meaning to me because of the meditation on the Luminous mysteries when you pray the rosary. The Luminous mysteries are on Thursday only.

The Mysteries are:

- The Baptism of Our Lord
- The Wedding at Cana
- The Proclamation of the Kingdom
- The Transfiguration
- The Institution of the Eucharist

The reason I was getting married was, so I could receive the Eucharist, *and* because I want to be married forever to Jeff in the Sacrament of Marriage, of course.

So, having the miracle of the water turned to wine at the Wedding at Cana *and* the Institution of the Eucharist on Thursday, our wedding day, was pretty special to me.

A few months before, I emailed my mom about all the things we had to do to get Sacramentally Married in the Catholic Church. She shared it with John and he said, "She is going through all of this just for Communion?" I think she may have been surprised at my response.

I sent her a link to a website, and maybe I educated her on the purpose of the Mass, the Body and Blood, Soul and Divinity present in the Eucharist and that it is the primary reason for Mass and the source and summit of our faith. I think that struck her pretty hard. She thanked me for forwarding it to her, and I think she was doing a bit of her own soul searching at that time.

I am so in love with the Eucharist that I have a vlog on this topic so you can see my face and my eyes as I talk about the remarkable gift I receive each time I go to Mass, our Lord, inside me growing and taking over.

Go to my website for my honest, heart-on-my-sleeve feelings about the Eucharist and the bible based Catholic teachings!

www.kendravonesh.com/eucharist

I told my mom about Jeff's decision not to go to confession, and therefore, he could not receive Communion at our wedding because he was not in a state of grace. My mom had not gone to confession since her wedding day, and she was 70 years old at this time.

I am not sure how we got on the topic, but my mom and I were talking about *her* going to confession, and I said I would go with her if she wanted. Maybe it all started because she wanted to receive Communion with me at my wedding. Maybe she felt bad that I would be the only one doing so, not quite sure.

We agreed to meet at the church for confession. I got there early, and out of all the gray-haired people in line, none of them was my mom. So, I decided, since the line was super long, that I would get in it. I kept looking behind me and no sign of her yet. It was now my time to go into the confessional, so I went in … still no sign of her.

On my way out, I happened to look up toward the end of the church toward the Narthex. Remember, St. Mary's in Huntley is massive. I was pretty sure that the gray-haired woman I spotted scurrying out the doors to the parking lot was my mom! I picked up the pace, almost to a jog, to get up the aisle and out the doors. Sure enough, it *was* my mom!

I yelled out, "Hey, Mom!!!" I think she knew it was me calling but she kept walking anyway. I yelled again, and she turned around. When I finally reached her, I told her I was in the confessional when she got there, and I asked why she was leaving. She said it was because she didn't see me.

"God-incidence" happened again. If I were two minutes longer, my mom would have been gone and who knows when or if she would have ever come back. We went back inside, and I got in line with her. She went in, and I waited in the pew doing my penance prayers. When she came out, she was SO quiet—eerily quiet.

I was quite uncomfortable sitting next to her. I thought, "Oh boy, is she mad at me for this?" I leaned over her, put my arms around her shoulder and whispered in her ear, "I love you, Mom."

After her penance prayers, we went to breakfast. We met Jeff there, who, of course, did not come join the fun at confession. When it was time to leave she walked over to me, looked me in the eye, hugged me and said, "Thank you for saving my life."

I am sure you can guess what I did next. Yep, I lost it. I bawled like a baby. My mother now goes to Mass regularly and goes to confession frequently. I hope that I had something to do with her soul seeking the Lord and all that comes with the Catholic Faith. We have gone to Mass a few times, I still like my parish in Elgin. I have a group of people that I know there, the ushers—one with whom I am very close with and hug/kiss on the cheek all the time, not to mention it is less packed with people.

But I should make more of an effort to go to Mass with her, I think it would be worth the crowds. But she likes to go Sunday night, I enjoy going on Sunday morning. We should really figure something out because she won't be here forever and what a great time to spend together receiving the Lord! Add that to the list.

A few days later was the night before the wedding, Jeff wasn't home yet, and I was starting to get worried. He was not answering my texts.

Perhaps he went to get a haircut or something? I started to pray that he was not in an accident.

Jeff finally responded to my text with a picture of a church, and he typed, "It didn't burn down!"

I was in shock. Did he ... did he ... did he go to *confession*?!?!?

I texted back with, "Does this mean what I think it means, did you go to confession?" He replied, "Yep" and I told him to be careful and hurry home.

Meanwhile, back in the bat cave, I proceeded to cry the ugliest cry I think I have ever cried. You know, the one with the most brutal face because you cannot control it, the one you don't want ANYONE to see. Yeah, that was me, the entire time until Jeff walked in the door.

When he got home, I ran to him, snotted all over his face and showered him with kisses, tears, and hugs.

After a few moments, I asked, "Sooooo, how was it?"

He said, "It felt awesome, I feel such a sense of relief, I am really happy I went!"

This was not a moment for "I told you so's" but I said it anyway. "Seeeee, what did I tell ya!?!? Amazing, right?"

I was in a state of shock for the rest of the night and thrilled that he was going to be in a state of grace with me, if for only a few days because I knew he wouldn't be going to Mass regularly. Unfortunately, he would go back in the mortal sin mode.

Yep, not going to Mass every week is a mortal sin. The Catholic Church strikes again, but Jeff was good to go for our wedding at least!

I believe that the Sacrament of Reconciliation (confession) goes hand in hand with the Sacrament of the Eucharist as the two sacraments without which, *I cannot live.*

I WOULD DIE—not just figuratively—I WILL DIE without confession or the Eucharist. Find out why I am so passionate about these two sacraments at:

www.kendravonesh.com/two-sacraments-that-make-me-catholic/

I am thrilled that my mother and my husband will be able to receive communion with me at our wedding tomorrow!

10

Three Times a Charm

It was "go time." We were about to get married!

We pulled up to the church, and my whole family was already there, except for my younger brother who had hockey (the story of a hockey family's life).

We spoke to the priest, got ourselves in order and went through a mini-like ceremony, we exchanged vows, and then suddenly it was over.

I looked at Father Chris and asked, "Aren't we going to receive Communion? My husband and mother have gone to confession specifically to receive Communion today after many decades, mind you."

Somewhere there was miscommunication ... and a big one at that.

My heart sunk, I wasn't sure what we were going to do. Father Chris felt horrible and said, "I am so sorry, hold on..." He walked to the Tabernacle, where the Consecrated Hosts are securely stored behind the altar and came to the three of us with "The Body of Christ" and we received the Lord.

I am pretty sure that counts, but in the end, I was okay with it either way! My mother and husband confessed, and my mother was a revert after that! A revert is a fallen away or non-practicing Catholic who returns to the faith and practices—religiously. I am a revert, too!

I have to share a brief story, before the ceremony, Father Chris came up to each of us standing in a line my Mom, then John, then Jeff, then me. He said to each of us, "Peace be with you" and all three of them responded with "And also with you." When he got to me, I said, "And with your spirit" he smiled and said, "Very good."

Boy, I sure remember the 'back row' Kendra when I said, "and also with you" and I am amazed at how far I have come in learning the faith.

We all went out and had a great dinner. For the most part, it was a very successful, family-filled night!

I couldn't wait to get to Mass on Sunday! I bounced out of bed, got dressed, and got there early so I could spend some time in prayer and express to the Lord how excited and unworthy I was to receive Him.

It seemed like the longest Mass ever. When it was time to get in line for Holy Communion I could feel my heart pounding, my body was vibrating like I was pumping electricity through it.

The Extraordinary Eucharistic Minister of Holy Communion (not a priest, but a layperson who was specially trained to distribute Communion) said, "The Body of Christ."

And I sang, "Aaaaamen!"

I turned to go back to my pew with … wait for it … wait for it … tears streaming down my face! And I didn't care who saw me cry.

When got to my pew, I knelt and put my face into my hands while I praised God for giving me the grace of faith and for being able to receive Him every day at Mass when I come to worship Him.

The Eucharist is so precious to me, I have put together a blog to show you to some of the most incredible Eucharistic miracles and other resources for the Body and Blood, Soul and Divinity present in the Eucharist on my website.

www.kendravonesh.com/eucharistic-miracles

I still don't understand, why did He give me this precious gift of accepting all the gifts the Catholic Church has to offer me?

I felt like a real Catholic … finally!

11

Mary, Mary, Mary

That should be read, "Marcia, Marcia, Marcia," like when Jan would whine about her older sister on the Brady Bunch. Sorry for anyone who doesn't get that reference, I guess I am showing my age!

For the next few months, God was still meeting me where I was, and I was still thirsting and devouring everything I could about the faith. I started to hear a lot about Mary. I struggled with it, to be honest.

Why would I go to Mary when I have a straight line to Jesus?

It took me some time to get the wax out of my ears to hear why we rely so much on our Blessed Mother for her intercession. But as soon as I cleared out the wax, it built up again, then cleared, then built up again. NOW I finally get it, and I was determined to continue to pray to her and for her help to get me closer to Jesus.

So, why Mary?

In a nutshell, Mary was completely obedient to God.

When the Archangel Gabriel came to announce to her and ask her to accept God's will and bear the child of God, she obeyed and allowed God to use her as His instrument. Mary wasn't exactly sure what was going to happen; she was young, she was pregnant and not married—a major "no-no," and she had to deal with all the judgment and disbelief of the people.

Mary was the first one to ask Jesus to do a miracle, the Wedding at Cana, turning the water into wine. Jesus, even though it was not his hour to do miracles yet, could not deny his mother's request. So, Mary looked at the servants and said, "Do whatever He tells you."

No single phrase sums up the obedience we must have for Jesus. "Do whatever He tells you." Meaning, live life on the narrow path, not the easy, happy-go-lucky, I will do what I want and what I believe path. In other words, "by *My* rules," Jesus says.

I am beginning to understand why there are all these rules in the Catholic Church, why there is a Pope, why we have governed the one church through hierarchy and tradition, and why the church is consistent throughout the world. The Mass, sacraments, and governance, is the same everywhere. That true repentance via the Sacrament of Reconciliation needs to be with a priest (representing Jesus), reciting our sins out loud and repenting with honest prayer, not just sitting in our houses saying, "Sorry, God, I screwed up," and all is forgiven. I mean, how easy is *that*? And since it is that easy, why not sin again and again.... all I have to do is think to myself "Sorry, God."

God knows what will make us happy and what we need to do to get into His Kingdom. We must get out of our "worldly ways" and start to chip away at ourselves and let go of some of the destructive behaviors we know and love so dearly.

But it is not easy, I am absolute proof of that!

Oh, did I mention that Mary was *sinless*? Let's think about that for a minute. SINLESS! I cannot even express in words, how is that even possible?

Lastly, on the Cross, Jesus gave us His Mother. She is OUR Mother! We should pray to her and ask for her intercession for all our petitions/needs/desires as well as for all sinners and for the conversion of our loved ones and the world. She is the closest one to Jesus, she is His Mother, she can help us get to Jesus—fast.

Have you ever asked someone to pray for you? Did they say, "No, you can go to Jesus yourself, you have a direct line to Him!" We ask for prayers all the time. It is the same with Mary and all the saints. Why *shouldn't* we ask for Mary's intercession to her Son who loves her so much that He assumed her into Heaven—body and soul?

Another thing I learned about Mary is there are all these names out there for her: Our Lady of Fatima, Mother of Perpetual Hope, Mystical Rose, Arc of the Covenant, and many others. Google titles of Mary, there are hundreds.

I did not know that all those names translate to MARY, which the Catholic faith fondly calls OUR LADY!

Mary has shown herself in many different forms to many different people throughout the world. You will also be amazed at how often she has APPEARED! These are called Marian apparitions. A Marian apparition is a reported supernatural appearance by the Blessed Virgin Mary. The vision of Mary is usually named after the town where it is reported, or on the nickname given to Mary on the apparition.

I was just recently reminded of her and how much I should revert to praying to her and the rosary, which has come and gone throughout the past five years. Many saints say the rosary is the weapon of our time and we should all pray a rosary a day, it is only 15 minutes of your day. I say this as much to myself as I do to you. I don't do it every day and I should, it's like putting on spiritual armor for the day.

During the fall of 2014, I heard a lot about Mary on the radio and on a few CDs from Father Michael Gaitley MJC who says, if you want to be holy, the quickest way to do that is to go to Mary and have her go to Jesus on our behalf.

Hmmmmm … really?

So, I got his book *33 Days of Morning Glory* and consecrated myself to Mary. I read each day. I must be honest, even though I read the book, I still wasn't "in it to win it" and slowly drifted away from Mary as my "go to."

November 9th (my birthday) was the day I started the book, and I finished on the Feast of Our Lady of Guadalupe. I did it again the same time in the Fall of 2015.

Unfortunately, it didn't really take hold, and my devotion to Mary faded away, and I started going back to Jesus directly and not praying the rosary or going to her with all my needs.

Then Father Michael Gaitley MJC caught my attention again, but this time with a DVD series "Divine Mercy in the Second Greatest Story Ever Told" where he uncovers St. Maximillian Kolbe, Our Lady of Fatima, St. John Paul II and their devotion to Our Lady. So, after I watched it, I started to understand how dedicated St. John Paul II was to Mary and Our Lady of Fatima, specifically. If you read about his assassination attempt, he said he was alive because she guided the bullet, it is all because of Mary.

The more I learn about Our Lady, the more I get it. I have a new dedication to praying the rosary and

.ng to her for my needs and for conversions of ..amily and friends. I have also heard about blessings by wearing The Miraculous Medal, I bought one for my mom and me a couple years ago. I just bought a "double set" a Cross and a Miraculous Medal on one chain during my $200 shopping spree at Marytown.

Wearing the Miraculous Medal under the sponsorship of the Blessed and Immaculate Virgin Mary is to pursue the conversion and growth in holiness of all people. Lord knows I need this—we ALL need this!

And lastly, Satan HATES Mary and despises the rosary because a human being is in such grace with God. When you pray the rosary, you are reciting 53 times of how much Our Lady is in God's graces. That is why it is said that the rosary is the weapon of our time and has changed history.

I just want to reiterate, we need *all* the help we can get to keep Satan away, and we ask people for prayers all the time.

Let's ask our Mother, angels, and saints for their help, it just makes sense. There is no more to it than that.

Catholics do not worship Mary, angels or saints. We do, however, hold them in the highest regard and know they had special graces here on earth, given by God, and we can ask for their help for ourselves and for others. When people ask me to pray for them, I go to all the above, *including* God.

Mary is a bit different than saints in that she is a sinless human who conceived Our Lord without losing her virginity. She requested to Jesus the very first miracle when it was *not* His hour to perform a miracle, but He did it anyway. Mommy asked, and He obliged. I want her to ask Jesus for things on behalf of ME!

Mary was there with Jesus through it all and on the cross, He gave her to us as Our Mother. She loves us and cares for us and walked with St. John The Apostle, Peter and the other Apostles when the church was created after His death. For those of you who are Scripture-based, remember that the Hail Mary prayer is based on Scripture, it is pulled from when God sent the Archangel Gabriel to ask her to give birth to Jesus.

Hail Mary, Full of Grace, The Lord is with Thee

Blessed Art Thou Among Women

And Blessed is the Fruit of Thy Womb, Jesus

Holy Mary, Mother of God, Pray for us Sinners

Now and at the Hour of Our Death

Amen

I share two awesome stories of Marian Apparitions—Our Lady of Fatima and the *only* one in the United States, Our Lady of Good Help at:

www.kendravonesh.com/visions-of-the-blessed-virgin-mary/

I mention Mary a lot, but I have also learned we can have the saints pray for us as well. I have a blog on the saints. I am fascinated that there are almost 10,000 saints in the Catholic Church! Each saint goes through a rigorous process that takes approximately 5-10 years for final approval to be Canonized as a saint. Part of that approval is Beatification *proving* that a miracle was performed through that saint. Then ANOTHER miracle is needed to be Canonized as a saint. I share a few of my favorite saints for these times and this culture, trust me, you will be able to relate.

www.kendravonesh.com/10k-saints-catholic-church/

12

I am Catholic, Hear Me Whisper

As I wore my cross, I found many people would ask me if I was Catholic. In the beginning, I was bold about it and said, "Yes, I am!"

Then a few people, some from other Christian faiths, asked why or how I could be Catholic with the priest scandals. That our faith doesn't "allow others into it" unlike other Christian faiths. Why not gay marriage? Some gay people I know have even asked me if I "Damn them to Hell?"

Whoa!

If you remember, in the beginning, before I was given the grace of the knowledge and acceptance of my faith, I also had issues with the Catholic teachings. Priest scandals, gay marriage, birth control, sex and living together before marriage, etc.

At this stage of my journey, I wasn't so clear on *how* to share my new-found faith and articulate why I was Catholic in a way that didn't make me sound like a hateful bigot. This shook me a little bit.

There are a lot of people who are not fans of the Catholic Church, and some are spiteful towards it. But the more I read, the more I learned and the more I believed. The teachings rang true to logic and the way I believe we should live, if I sat back and was honest with myself, the teachings made sense to me. Even though I know how difficult it is to achieve this level of morality, *it still made sense to me.* I just needed to learn how best to communicate this *with love.* I don't shun people who live contrary to the faith—it is quite the opposite. I chose to live according to my faith, this is my choice. Even though we may not agree, I do not stop loving you or caring for you.

I want to be sure you hear me loud and clear. I love *everyone.* I may not agree with everyone, but I love everyone.

And I have lived immorally! I wish I had lived my life differently. I exhibited no self-mastery, no self-control, I went after what I wanted, and I overindulged on all of life's pleasures! According to the Catholic Church—I was living in mortal sin. The Catholic Church has a *super high bar* that is more than difficult to achieve. Our secular culture is so focused on the individual that we should be happy so do what makes you happy regardless of the cost. But the Catholic Church also has incredible mercy in the forgiveness of sins to counteract the high bar of morality, thankfully, through the Sacrament of

Reconciliation so we can start over and try again to strive for the high bar.

And when I started to learn what Jesus was teaching us about how we need to live it really made me think. What in the heck was I doing? I need to start living differently, or I may be heading straight to Hell! I wish there was a switch that I turned, and all my sinful living went away. I am just like St. Augustine—"Save me, Lord ... but not just quite yet!"

It is so much easier to live life as a full-blown sinner, all about me, doing what I want when I want and how much I want, me, me, meeeeeeee! And I certainly I wasn't all that wild about changing how I was living. But when I started to change and started to pay attention to how I was living my life, the change was not only easier but my life became so much richer!

I am *nowhere* near where I want to be regarding living my life as the best witness of Jesus, but I strive to be better every day.

And when I shared my faith, and people saw the changes in me, they were genuinely interested in what was causing it. I have been amazed how many people are searching for more meaning in their lives or for some sanity as life can be overwhelming most of the time.

I completely get it and know how you feel because I am still challenged with living how I want instead of how He wants me to live, and I will struggle with this until I die. Just know that God has a plan for you, your unique life and how best to use you and the talents He gave you and only you. All you need to do is just *ask* Him to meet you where you are, He knows your deepest needs and darkest secrets, He knows you better than you know yourself and He has *all* the answers. And He will be there in your darkest moments to help you as I was going to find out soon enough.

13

The First Curve Ball

At the beginning of 2015, there were some changes at my job, including new leadership that I wasn't crazy about. I decided that I should "put myself out there" to see if there were other opportunities where I could benefit, learn, and grow.

Ironically, a recruiter contacted me, and I was very interested in the position he was looking to fill. So, I decided to throw my hat in the ring and go through the process. During this time, I was close to the Perpetual Adoration Chapel, so I spent a LOT of time there praying that I would get the position so that I could leave my job on my terms and learn a new industry.

One thing I always ended with after my "begging and pleading" for the job was, "Only if it is your will, Lord." I had finally learned that the Lord will grant our prayers if it is His will for us, not our selfish will. Sometimes we will align, but ultimately,

He knows what is best for us, especially when we think we do, too.

I finally had ears to hear in the Our Father 'THY will be done.' I have recited that prayer thousands of times and I only really heard THY in the prayer a few months after my journey began. Amazing I hadn't really heard it in the past. Lots of wax I tell you, Q-Tip?

It was a long interview process. It drew out for a couple of months between another candidate and me. I felt somewhat confident but knew that the candidate I was up against was much more technical than me. My insecurities flooded my soul, I still wanted the role, but the broken record of "you are not good enough, smart enough, technical enough" started playing.

One day in Adoration, my head was saying, "Maybe this isn't the role for me, maybe something else would be a better fit?" It was so bizarre. I went from begging and pleading as if this job was the *only* one for me and I needed it to survive to "eh, no big deal if it doesn't happen" in my hour with Jesus in Adoration.

It was at that moment when I understood how important it is to *listen* to God in *silence*. Thoughts fill your head and your heart and guess who puts them there sometimes? Jesus! The key is to know which are your thoughts, which are Jesus' thoughts, and which are Satan's.

Turns out, I didn't get the job, and I was not surprised or even disappointed! I remember telling Jeff that I sensed it and that I thought that Jesus was trying to show me that in Adoration. I felt a sense of calmness take over. We were okay with it, and I kept plugging away at my current job but kept my eyes out for new opportunities.

Then, it happened. I was let go from my job about a month later.

I knew that it was most likely going to happen due to leadership changes. It was gratifying to hear my boss say that it was not because of performance, but just what I suspected, it was because of our leadership style differences. We were completely opposite in our approach.

But that didn't stop me from resenting him. I was pretty ticked off, and I couldn't quite get over the fact that it happened. It was hard for me to let go of the hatred I felt for him. Yes, I said hatred. I just didn't like him. In my opinion, he was untrustworthy, stifled creativity from team members, and he didn't communicate well with anyone. I equate him as a dictator who wanted "yes people" under his belt. Again, opposite to my style.

I had horrible dreams about him, and every time I thought of him, disdain crept into my head and flooded my psyche. It was like poison, and I had no antidote!

Low and behold, I heard a lot about forgiveness not only on the radio but in Bible verses and the Gospel as well. They struck a chord.

If I do not forgive and pray for this man, God would NOT forgive ME!

Let me put it another way. I go to confession … a LOT! (Thank you, Father Chris, for having confession right before Sunday Mass, by the way, makes it so easy to go weekly!) I feel great when I go, and it helps me live better and with purpose. I have more compassion and love flowing throughout my soul and my actions every time I leave the confessional.

It also reminds me of the grace God has for me, He forgives all my sins. I don't go into the confessional and say, "Boy, I sure hope God forgives me." I *expect* God to forgive me. And He also expects me to learn and change and not to sin anymore.

That is where the rubber meets the road for me. I must change, I cannot keep going into that confessional and then leave and repeat, rinse, repeat the same sins! What is THAT all about? And how can I expect Him to forgive me unconditionally, no matter what, and me not forgive in the same way? As a matter of fact, I am called to forgive everyone and love everyone as my neighbor. Why is it so hard to do that?

I prayed for the grace to forgive this man. It took me about 7 months to sincerely forgive, pray, and wish the best for him. Now, I don't resent this guy, I actually reflect on the good times we had and hope he is doing well.

I have a much different view of people and the crosses we carry and the mistakes we ALL make. We are human, we are not perfect and will never be perfect. I am now praying for everyone. That is what God wants us to do. It is October 2017 as I write, and I am praying for the soul of the man who shot all those people at the concert in Las Vegas.

I am reminded of the part of the rosary prayer, "Oh my Jesus, forgive us our sins, save us from the fires of Hell, lead all souls to Heaven, especially those most in need of thy mercy." This is what we need to do, for ourselves and for the salvation of the world, pray for sinners. And I am one of them!

I can't help but wonder how I would have handled the let down of not getting that job opportunity and being let go from my existing job if I didn't have my faith.

This is why I was compelled to tell my story because I am growing in faith, hope, love and my trust in Jesus to guide me every step of the way. I have a sense of peace and more compassion than I have ever had in my life these past few years. I am so much more joyful and appreciate all the beauty around me that I ignored most of the time. I cannot stop smiling a huge smile to everyone to pass on my joy and happiness. I honestly can't help it, seriously, I am bursting!

And I am not afraid to die, oddly enough, I am looking forward to it but not until God takes me. While I am on this planet, I need to help everyone enrich their lives through faith and prayer. How great would it be to not worry anymore? Worry, why pray? Pray, why worry? A shoe-shine guy, DeMarco, I met told me that, and it stuck because it is so true.

I guarantee I would not have accepted losing my job as a blessing or saw the suffering as a sacrifice to God without my faith. And I certainly would have freaked out about what my next gig would be and would have spent many a sleepless night worrying and trying my hardest to figure it out, alone. I probably wouldn't be able to move my neck or have any teeth left in my mouth either!

Looking back, I am SO happy that I didn't get that job. And I also found it a blessing that I departed from that company and the manager with whom I didn't align.

Even while I was in the midst of it, smack dab in the muck, I was sure that God had a plan for me. I knew it. The problem is I didn't know what that plan WAS! All I knew was I had to trust in Him completely, live in the present moment arm and arm together—ONE DAY AT A TIME.

But I am not really good at doing that. I am a planner. I am a worrier. I am a doer. I am a whack job! Let's face it, I grew up in IT where we planned out our projects months in advance, I knew my annual budget and projects, and I had a three-year strategy, blah, blah, blah. I practically lived my life in the future.

But because of my faith, I still believed I needed to take this day by day and trust that Jesus had a plan. I had to say that to myself a thousand times a day, and my faith still wavered a bit. "I believe, Lord, help my unbelief." I still struggle today to live in the present and to trust that God is with me at all moments. I know this to be true, but I am my own worst enemy, my thoughts are my nemesis. But I try, oh how I try. It's a journey people, all I can ask is to make progress and give myself a break, I am human.

While in the process of finding my next gig, I was already committed to being on a CIO panel at a software company's conference. I let them know that I was no longer with my organization and asked if they still wanted me on stage. Not only did they want me on stage, they asked me if I would come early to meet with their sales team to help them sell to CIO's and to host a Women's Executive Luncheon.

What the heck, why not? I don't have a full-time gig, it is in San Francisco, and they are paying all expenses. I was in!

I had no idea what would happen next. I attended the CEO's keynote, and throughout the three-day conference I felt the vibe of the culture, saw the vision of the future and was "pimped" around to meet all the executive leadership team. The Global EVP of Sales wanted me to join the company, so I could evangelize as an executive advisor and brand ambassador to customers and prospects.

They flew me back out to San Francisco for a series of interviews the week after the conference, created a position for me and made me an offer a week later. I had another offer to consider from a local consulting company with a great culture, but quite a different role.

It is sad to say, but I thought, "What would people think of me if I took this role? I am sure they are expecting me to be a CIO. Would I lose status in their eyes, in my eyes, in my husband and family's eyes?"

After a lot of consideration weighing all the pros and cons with Jeff, I decided to join the software company and try out being an Executive Advisor.

14

My Divine Intervention

In about a week I would be flying to San Francisco to attend Boot Camp for my new role as Executive Advisor (aka Evangelist/Brand Ambassador). This was going to be a very new way of living for Jeff and me.

We talked about how much travel there would be for me and that he would be responsible for taking care of the dogs and one of them was pretty sick. The dog had a growth on her face that was affecting her eating. I was blending up her food, and she could eat it out of her bowl, then I was hand-feeding it to her. She was still moving well, eating, drinking, and pooping okay. Sorry, but that is an important point. I didn't think it was time for her to be put down yet.

The inside of her cheek started to bleed because the tumor was growing in her mouth and when chewing food, it tore itself open.

On Sunday, July 5, 2015, I drove to the vet to pick up some antibiotics, it was a full bottle and not cheap. The last thing I was thinking about was putting her down before I left for San Fran that Saturday. I did, however, pray a lot for her health.

That evening she was shaking a bit while standing. I prayed in bed that night, asking God for a sign, was now the time to put her down? I mean, come on, I just picked up a full bottle of meds for her!

On Monday morning something told me to Google "signs of when you should put down a dog," and my 14-year-old dog had 7 of the 10. I felt, in my heart, it was time. I emailed Jeff the link and asked him what he thought. He thought the decision should have been made a while ago, but he needed me to get to that on my own. I know it was God who made me realize, in such a short timeframe, that it was her time.

The good thing was our vet comes to your house to euthanize your pet, so they don't have to be under undue stress going to the office. I asked when they could come to the house. They said, "3:00 tomorrow, but you need to come here and get some medication that will sedate her and give it to her an hour before the vet arrives."

Tuesday morning, I headed back to the vet to get the medicine to make her death more comfortable. On the way there, I decided to call the local church, to see if the priest could come and bless her.

It was only a few minutes away. The priest was tied up in a meeting and needed to call me back, I was sobbing on the phone talking to the lovely woman who answered my call.

I arrived at the vet to pick up the meds. They were very sweet and wished me well and would pray for us.

I got in the car and thought that I better get myself back to the house in case the priest could come over right away to bless her. Then I thought, "But I am 15 minutes away from the Perpetual Adoration Chapel, maybe I should go sit with God for a while?"

This was a tough decision.

I could miss the priest by going to the Adoration Chapel because it was 50 minutes from the lake house. Jeff was working from there that day. Even though *he* would be there, *I* wouldn't be there. After I agonized a bit, I decided to take my chances and go to Adoration.

I pulled into the parking lot of St. Mary's in Huntley, which is always full. I was about to pull into a parking spot on the left when a white SUV pulled up and into the spot, so they were facing outward and could just pull forward to leave.

Hmph—that was *my* spot.

So, I went around to the other aisle and parked in a space across from that SUV.

As I got out of my car, I checked out the person who was in that SUV now walking toward the church.

Hmmmm ... she looked familiar ... I thought I recognized that hair and that walk.

"Mom?" I shouted. She turned around. IT WAS HER!

I ran to her, bawling like crazy and hugging her so tight I am sure she found it hard to breathe.

"What are you doing here?" I asked.

"I am going to confession," she replied.

I explained to her my decision to go to Adoration instead of going home and that I was pulled to the church instead.

She explained that she had meant to go to confession for a few weeks, but decided to go that day. She told John to go to his doctor's appointments by himself because she needed to go *today*.

We both knew it was Divine Intervention. There was no "chance" that this could have happened. This was, by far, one of the biggest "God-incidences" of my life.

There we were crying and hugging in the church parking lot, it was insane. We both knew and felt the same about seeing each other.

We both went to confession that day, and I spent some time in Adoration.

On my back way to the lake, I was listening, as always, to Relevant Radio. Go Ask Your Father was on, so I took a chance to call Monsignor Swetland to ask him about putting my dog down and if that was right in the eyes of the church and if animals went to Heaven. I got through, he explained to me that we need to be sure that animals do not suffer, and he believes, although it isn't written, that all of God's creatures go to Heaven, or something like that. I felt much better and that I was doing the right thing.

About 30 seconds after I hung up with Monsignor Swetland, I got a call from the woman at the parish by the lake house. She said that Father Sean could come at 2:00!

REALLY?

It was about 12:45. That gave me about an hour to sit with my dog before I had to give her the medicine so she'd still be "awake" to hear the blessing.

When I got home, I told Jeff about seeing my mom at church. He got pretty emotional about it, and he started tearing up as I shared the "God-incidence." I told him about my call with Monsignor and that the priest would come and bless her, too.

It was a rough hour, I sat on the floor next to her bed and just looked at her, talked about all the great times and that I would see her in Heaven. The priest came and blessed her, I recorded the whole thing, and I was very much at peace. Jeff, on the other hand, lost it big time.

I firmly believe it was my faith that kept me together and God who lined up everything that day. I knew it... I felt it... she would be going to God. I hope Jeff felt it, too.

Today is October 3rd, 2017. As I am typing this chapter, I am going to take my other dog (her sister) to church in one hour (if I can pull my snotty, blubbering self together—you should see the mess of a woman I am right now).

Today is a pet blessing in front of the church in honor of St. Francis of Assisi, the Patron Saint of Animals. They usually do this on the 4th, which is St. Francis' Feast Day, but they had to do it a day early this year.

Time to take a break, pull myself together and get my dog blessed.

15

How Can Anyone Be Lukewarm?

After an emotional few days, I was getting ready to depart for the 10-day trip to San Francisco for Boot Camp.

This is where my faith and prayer life suffered a bit.

We played hard and worked hard. I traveled all the time, wined, dined, and then partied it up with all the reps and sales support teams. We are talking many late nights (or early mornings) and *many* hangovers.

Even though things were cooling off for me prayer-wise, I was still going to Mass every Sunday, even when I traveled internationally. I even went to confession at Notre Dame!

Another way to pass the time walking through the airport, on the plane, or while I was delayed was listening to my audio Bible and free speeches I downloaded from Scott Hahn.

A quick plane story for you. Jeff and I were going on vacation. I seem to get stuck in the middle seat, and he gets the aisle when we travel together. I was reading Matthew Kelly's *Rediscovering Catholicism*, and the guy sitting next to me asked, "So, what is the book you are reading?"

"Uuuuuuhhhhh…" my whispering Catholic voice was struggling to speak. So, I just turned the book around and showed it to him.

He said, "Oh, I thought it looked familiar, I have read that, it is pretty good." Then we talked a little bit about the faith and then went about our business. I remember freaking out to Jeff about the fact that we were both Catholic and what were the chances of us reading the same book and talking about it, etc. "God-incidence."

There were many times where I sat next to people on the plane, and my faith came up in conversation. Surprisingly, most people were very interested, and none of the encounters were rude or went south, which is why I am slowly but surely learning to ROAR rather than whisper about my faith and keeping my it to myself.

It is just taking a bit of time and more confidence and commitment on my part. And I think I can read people. I am pretty sure when they are or are not interested in what I am saying. So, I act accordingly.

I began to have some serious, faith-filled conversations with some co-workers as well. It was nice to find this in others, especially with people I worked with, so we could relate on a different level. I feel not only was I an evangelist for the company's software but also on the Catholic faith at times.

But I also heard from a few peers, "You are such a dichotomy. You profess your faith, yet you are the biggest partier and potty mouth I have ever known!"

Hmph, yeah, that was pretty much me.

That year was hard on my liver, I gained a lot of frequent flyer miles and cellulite while my selfless husband spent many a night home with our dog. I found that my faith, while still there, was taking a back seat.

Let's face it, who can pray at night and examine your day when you are pretty much passed out? And in the morning, while I might play the rosary on my smartphone or listen to morning prayers I would be fighting through my yawns and in some cases headaches and plain exhaustion.

I remember thinking at the beginning of my faith journey, "How could ANYONE lose their faith and become lukewarm? I am on fire, and I love it. I will never let God take a backseat, I will always seek Him deeply every day."

Then, life gets in the way, priorities get out of whack. And the more we push Him down, the more we fall back into our worldly ways.

I started to notice that I was drinking a LOT, even when I was not traveling. It was February of 2017 when I sat down with Jeff and said, "Honey, I cannot remember the last time I haven't had a glass of wine either at home or on the road. I was thinking about quitting drinking altogether for a while to see if I CAN quit."

As much as he hates the "flavors of the month" I come up with, he was in for this one. He said, "Hmmm, this will be interesting because you have quite a lot of events this month." I replied, "Don't I know it, but it's a good test."

It was challenging, at first, not to drink. People then knew I wasn't drinking even though they gave me flack, it didn't deter me.

I was back in my hotel room at respectable hours, I had time to reflect and pray and actually remembered the conversations I had the night before! I also realized that there were plenty of other people at these events who were not drinking either.

I felt a bit of empowerment flowing through me. Being able to say, "No thanks" was an enlightening experience for me. I sound all proud here, but don't let me fool you, I did pray to God to help me and give me strength not to have a drink.

Trust me, there were times when I thought, "I'll just have a couple..." And that means more than two for me.

We didn't drink for about a month. Jeff lost quite a few pounds. We could have just quit drinking vs. the cleanse a few years back! I started seeing some healthy changes in myself as well.

I examined my entire lifestyle, looking at my eating habits and how much I was working out ... or not. I decided to begin to live a Keto-lifestyle. Keto is high fat, high protein, and very low carbs. I dropped a lot of weight and was working out when I could, but I wasn't obsessed with it.

I felt like I finally got a hold of myself and was in control of all aspects of my life professionally, spiritually, personally and physically. I was feeling great about my life, and I was balancing it all nicely.

Then a few more bombs started to drop.

Here we go again. Silly me, I have *no* control of my life. Haven't I learned that yet?

16

Second, Third, Fourth Curve Balls

I was sitting in a manager's meeting in San Francisco when I received an email from my husband saying that we got hit with 7 inches of rain overnight.

Unfortunately, our lake house is in a floodplain— one of the lowest parts of the Chain O Lakes. We knew this when we bought it, and since this is not our permanent home, we figured we always have a place to move to if necessary.

Even though we had four feet of water in our yard, the blessing is that we did not have the water reach into our house or wick up to the rafters and damage our foundation. We had 4 weeks where we couldn't move in and had quite the clean up when we finally did.

This happened a few months before the hurricanes and the flooding in Texas, Louisiana, Florida, and the Caribbean. So, in comparison, we were VERY blessed. I can't even complain about our situation after seeing what those people had to deal with, what they lost, and how they will continue to suffer for the near future.

Then Jeff's ex-wife passed away. The boys (20 and 23 years old at the time) were at her bedside at the hospital along with Jeff and her husband. The boys had to make the difficult decision to let her pass due to many reasons of which I will not go into to respect her privacy.

I, of course, was on the road when I got the call.

I was in disbelief, she was so young, she was a fabulous mother, and the boys should not have to deal with this at their age. I kept thinking about all the moments she would miss and couldn't really console my heart.

It was a rough week. We moved one of the boys in with us and we tried to get on with life, which would never be the same. I tried to be the best mother I could be to them.

I have been in their lives since they were 5 and 8 and now I needed to be more involved. I wanted to make sure they knew they could come to me, tell me anything, and ensure we would continue to see them as often as possible. They were super close to their mom. As I said, she was awesome.

One of the boys recently got a promotion, and the other was getting out of the restaurant business, interviewing for a corporate position so he could have time to see family and friends and not work those crazy hours. He got the job, and I did my best to make sacrifices and pray for him *instead* of me.

We have seen each other quite often, and I pray that we make some positive memories for the upcoming holidays as this is the first without their loving mother.

The last bomb came when I was informed the software company I was working for had to eliminate the position that I loved. The Executive Advisor position had been created for me, where I shared my story with passion. I built solid, long-term relationships with hundreds of executives, customers, prospects and their teams. But my time had come, and I understood the decision to eliminate my role.

While I knew it was not going to last forever, I realized that I was good at what I did, and I enjoyed it very much. I have the personality to engage and connect with people quickly and gain their trust as I guided them along the way. I was never "selling" anything, and I believe they could sense that. I was trying to help my customers succeed, and I was genuinely concerned for their wellbeing.

This happened in September of 2017. Now I am back in the market and trying to figure out *again* what I want to be when I grow up.

There is this nagging inner tug that is shouting, "Don't go back to what you were doing…" But that is what I have done in the recent past, and I have made good money doing it.

I immediately went back into 'networking mode' like I did before. I booked my calendar with some of my closest friends and colleagues, with whom I could be myself and banter around some possible future career options. I was more than overwhelmed when each person I met thought I could do any number of things. My most recent role opened many different opportunities for me.

Some said I should consult on my own, others said I should be a speaker about something I am passionate about, others suggested a stand-up comedian, facilitator, or a TV or radio host!

Really?

I extended my meetings to executive recruiters and other people in my network. This was my attempt at a "fall back" plan, I can always be a CIO because I know that job.

I then decided to reach out to a close friend, whom I have known for decades. He had gone through quite the transformation over the past few years. He was a CFO, then went into a sales role selling financial services, and then went through a significant personal change and got divorced.

He realized sales wasn't his calling, so he picked up his entire life, left his extensive network in Chicago, and moved to southern California. When he did that, I was perplexed. Ballsy sums it up for me.

It had been a while since we had spoken, and he was flailing a bit. After being in California for about a year, he wasn't much closer to finding his purpose in life. He said he was working with a life coach.

Turns out he was in the beginning stages of working with her and wasn't exactly sure how things would go, but he figured he wasn't making a lot of headway on his own so why not try this.

When we reconnected a couple of months later, he was a different person! His attitude and his life were all heading in the right direction. He found his meaning and purpose in life and wants to help others do just that. He started his life-coaching business, Dreambridge Coaching.

After a month or so of networking and feeling this gnawing, sick to my stomach feeling that I would go back into an operational IT role, I thought I would ask for his help. Why not help him out by hiring him? He knows me really well; I could cry with him versus a coach I wasn't familiar with, and I really needed some guidance.

I think it is worth noting my coach was raised Catholic but was not practicing. Although he is very spiritual and many of the things he says rang true in the Catholic Faith and resonated with me, he is not about Catholicism (even though his mother keeps on him to come back). His mom sent him *Resisting Happiness*, a book by Matthew Kelly, and I also texted him the link to get a free copy as well. Too funny that his mom already sent it to him.

One of the things he taught me is that I need to slow down. I need to stop "doing," start "listening," and to take the time to sit in silence, hearing what my soul says but he re-phrases that to me as "the soft-spoken words and signs of God." He meditates. He knows all about my faith, so he ties everything to that for me.

My mother has also said that I need to slow down and take my time. She even went as far as saying, "Who are you trying to impress?"

I have repeated that phrase to myself many times. Who AM I trying to impress? Why should I care what people think of me and what I do for a living, how much money I make, what status I have in a company?

But that is easier said than done, this is how I have always been. I have continuously cared TOO much about what people think, and it has driven a lot of my behavior throughout my life. But at that moment, I was more concerned about what my husband was thinking.

In my screwed-up head, I believed he wanted me to shut up and go get a job— and a good paying one at that. I believed he thought work was not supposed to be something you love, that's why it is called a job. I believed he was thinking I was wasting my time with this life-coach thing and possibly concerned it would take me in a more faith-filled direction. I believed he didn't want me to take any time to find my meaning and purpose in life and that I only had a couple decades to continue working so 'get after it.'

That's what I thought—until I talked to him.

My husband is the most loving and considerate person I know. "Love thy neighbor" is how he truly lives. He would do anything for you and is a super hard worker at everything he does. He is my moral compass as well. He'll say comments to me after I make some snide remark about someone on TV or say something completely inappropriate or contrary to my faith. "Well, looks like you need to get back to church or go to confession there, missy!" He makes me a better person.

So, when I said that I needed his support and to have no time limits on my next phase and for him not to judge me, he said the most perfect thing to me. He made a God-like comment to me, "We will take it day by day." And supported me completely.

I realize that I am truly blessed to have him in my life. I also recognize that he did not marry the woman I am today. He married this wild child, lover of all the comforts this world can offer. Then I found my faith and started to change a little (not as much as I realize I need to as I have mentioned).

He is supportive and is proud of me. He could surely resent me and hate this "Jesus thing" and want his old wife back! For example, we were at a friend's vacation home and were hanging out in September. Somehow, as always, my faith journey came up in conversation.

Jeff said to the other couple, "You know she is more and more into her faith and I am really very proud of what she is doing and who she is becoming." I about fell over. Really? You are? That is so cool! So, why don't you come join me?

But I also know that I am not the Holy Spirit and cannot push him into faith. And you know I pray all the time for his conversion. I hope one day it will happen.

I think if he were into faith with me we could volunteer and give back together. I wouldn't feel guilty doing that alone because he is at home without me. I *actually* enjoy my husband and want to spend every moment with him. So, volunteering without him isn't nearly as appealing to me.

The next day at our friend's house, we had dinner with another couple. We talked about faith and Catholicism, specifically. We had a bunch of drinks, and everyone was feeling pretty good.

I started getting a bit raunchy, and my girlfriend said, "Here you are this Catholic faith-filled person yet you're talking like this and swearing like a truck driver."

That hit me like a ton of bricks.

Honestly, as I was saying the things I was saying I was thinking, "Hmmm, this is not congruent with you being a good witness of Jesus." Then I thought, "But this is what people expect of me, who I have always been, will they like me if I am NOT this way?"

That seems like a lot to go through your head when you're drinking and talking, but it all did. It goes with the other feedback from people over the past couple years and the "you are a dichotomy" comment.

I completely understand why they would think that and it really devalues and cheapens everything I say about the faith. I am a walking, breathing, drinking, swearing oxymoron, or maybe just a moron.

On our drive back home the next morning, I told Jeff how her comment really got to me, that I really needed to be a better example.

He was very sympathetic and said, "Honey, you have 42 years of living like that and only the past 4 years of faith, give yourself a break."

17

YOU May Be the Only Gospel
People See or Hear

In true form, I began to hear all over the radio and in the daily readings that we must deny ourselves, pick up our crosses, live on the narrow path, and go through the narrow door.

I have heard it many times before, but God finally took the wax out of my ears so that I can finally hear.

I now understand what it means to deny myself and follow Him. It signifies that I must do what He tells me to do, as Mary plainly stated to the servants at the Wedding at Cana, "Do whatever He tells you." Regardless of whether I want to or if others want me to, I must deny myself. Now, what does that mean?

I must not give into doing whatever my silly little self wants to do.

It is 12:30 on a Tuesday afternoon. I could have a drink or smoke. I could take a nap and NOT focus on this book. I could eat a whole pie, cheeseburger and fries.

But would any of those actions be helpful to me?

Matthew Kelly and my good friend and life coach, Jeff Baker both have a purpose in life to help people be the best versions of themselves.

I could also shy away from shining like the light of the Lord because it is uncomfortable to defend or isn't popular in today's culture. The Apostles went out to spread the word across the world with no money, one coat, a pair of shoes—pretty much nothing.

That is what Christians are called to do as well, pick up their cross, and follow Him no matter how people react to you, or in some extreme cases, if they kill you!

I could also decide to go back to a job that pays great but has no real purpose or meaning to me. I could take the easy way out and do what is expected from others because I have 'been there, done that' and it would be familiar to me rather than to do something I have *never* done before. I could live in fear because I am scared to try something new.

I have made it to a place in my life where I can take the time to do some soul searching and figure out what I was made to do, and not paid to do.

It is time for me to put my money where my mouth is and trust that God has a plan for me. I need to take each day as it comes, live in the present, and pray to increase my faith, hope, and love. I need to reassure myself that discerning a professional vocation will be in God's time, not mine.

I cannot put a timebox on this and expect it to be done like a project. I have already tried to do that, unsuccessfully. I need to sit in quiet peace and listen to the thoughts God puts in my head and fight off every self-doubting thought from the King of Lies, Satan. I need to put God *first* in my life.

That all sound great, but hard to do. Each and every day, every hour, every minute, I need to reach out to God and ask for his help. It is hard to remember that I am not in this alone.

I also need to make some sacrifices to show that I am worthy of His help. I need to ACT like a Catholic and live life on the narrow path, which means following ALL the rules.

God gave us this plan and way to live because He knows the best way to live with peace and joy. He knows true happiness is not what the almighty dollar buys or what the alcohol and drugs make us feel for the short moments we use them. We should have charity toward others and be love itself.

It is funny that I am finally seeing this for the first time and understanding what this means to me. I must let go of my old self, my old habits, my past behaviors and be a beaming beacon of love and compassion. I must serve and help others.

I can admit that I did not want to change my life. I still struggle with changing it as I type those words right now, too. As I said, I loved my life, my worldly ways. It is easier to live that way, in some respects, and harder in others *knowing* what I know about Jesus and how He wants us to live.

To be completely honest, sometimes I wish I didn't know any of this and could go back to the way I lived before, all about me. I know exactly how to live that way! And it is super easy to do.

But I am also happy that I do believe in Jesus as Our Savior and know what I need to do to live in eternity in Heaven and stay FAR away from the burning flames in Hell. I am grateful He gave me the grace of faith—now, what am I going to do with it?

I know I can no longer be a walking contradiction.

I would like to thank God for giving me the grace to have ears to FINALLY hear that! I need to pick up my cross and follow Him. I must deny myself and give Him the chisel, so He can chip away at the 47 years of 'worldly living' and reveal the true disciple and saint I should be and to spread the word to the ends of the earth—or just right here in my own community!

18

Community—It's Not So Bad

I still like to keep to myself at Mass.

I choose to go to the early Mass on Sunday because there are typically fewer families with children, it is less crowded, and I feel like I can keep to myself. It's not that I don't like children but sometimes it can be a bit distracting.

As you know, I pretty much roll out of bed, put my hair in a ponytail, skip the makeup, arrive "just in time," and I am out the door after the final blessing and before the closing hymn is over.

Truth be told, I have even left a couple times with the Eucharist in my mouth right after I received Him. I am *not* proud of that fact.

Perhaps if I dressed better and "did myself up," I might be more social, more confident, and want to talk to people? But that means I have to get up an hour and a half earlier! What about my sleep?

I have been noticing that God keeps putting people in my way.

I think He is testing my ability to love my neighbor as myself. And to teach me that church is a community and He wants us to live like a family.

For example, I went to Marytown/The Shrine because they have confession daily. It had been a while since I went. I try to go every two weeks, at a minimum every month. I was pushing a month and a week at this point.

After confession, I figured I would stay for Mass at noon. I was in and out of the confessional quickly and had plenty of time to grab a seat in one of the first pews. I sat on the end, as if I put a sign over me saying, "Hey, do not sit here, I want to be at the end of the pew, so I can get out. Go sit somewhere else!"

I began praying the rosary before Mass started because I had committed to myself that I would incorporate more daily time with God.

I had not made it through the first decade when a woman came and sat down about a foot from my right.

My initial reaction was, "Really? You can't pick another place to sit out of ALL these empty seats?" Then I got an overwhelming feeling of calmness and a smile came over my face. "That's a good one, God … I know what you are doing."

So, I continued on with the rosary.

I was on the 4th decade of the rosary when another woman came up on my left and asked, "Can I sit here?" I responded, "Sure," and slid over from my seat on the end of the pew to make room for her. But I couldn't slide over too far because the other woman was sitting next to me on my right. I am now the meat in this faith-filled sandwich!

All of the sudden some bells started to ring, and I looked at my watch, it was 11:45. The Mass wasn't supposed to start until 12:00. What is going on?

The priest started speaking at the podium, and the people around me started responding. I had no idea what they were saying, and I felt like a complete idiot.

The woman who just sat down next to me handed me her booklet, pointed to the part we were reading and said, in what I think is a Polish accent, "And when we are done with this part go back and read this line." Then she got up and walked over to the table on the side of the church and grabbed a few more of those booklets.

Apparently, she saw a few other clueless folks around us and she handed them the booklets. I could now follow along. When she sat back down, I whispered humbly in her ear with absolute sincerity, "Thank you SO much!"

And the woman to my right was one of those people who talk loudly, which was a good thing because there were some responses that were not in the book and I was able to stumble along with her.

She was a tiny Asian woman with a lot of might and passion for her faith.

The appreciation I felt filled my soul that day. It turned out the Mass was *packed* as it was a Blue Mass for all the first responders. I was feeling warm and fuzzy with these super faith-filled women next to me who wanted to be in the front row. I was honored to be with them as they deserved to be there a heck of a lot more than I did!

I was grateful to God for putting them in my way that day. I think I was getting His message, love thy neighbor, *even at Mass.*

The priest who was playing the organ and singing was amazing. He was a young man, probably early to mid-twenties if I had to guess. I wanted to tell him how awesome he was, but he left before I was able to.

At the end of Mass, I did NOT get up and run out. I sat and finished the last decade of the rosary because I was cut off from doing that when they started the daily prayers.

When I was done praying I had to go find the ladies room before the commute home. On my way, I saw the priest who had played the organ, and I decided this was my chance.

I went up to him and said, "You are amazing, your playing and voice are just beautiful!" He responded with an angelic voice, oozing with appreciation, "Thank you so much, what is your name?"

I was kind of shocked and sputtered, "Kendra."

He said softly, "I will pray for you, Kendra."

I had to fight back my tears. I was feeling so unworthy to receive this priest's prayers as there are so many others who need them. I choked out the words, "Oh my, that is really not necessary, but thank you!"

I reached out and touched his arm. I am one of those people who touches people a lot when I am talking to them. Even when I first meet them, which probably freaks some people out, but I think it helps with connecting faster. I don't think I could stop doing it if I tried.

I headed back home pretty happy that I spent some time with God today. My coach suggested that I clear my calendar, meaning no networking. I decided I could go to daily Mass that week as well. I did as I was told and didn't book any networking appointments. I kept busy organizing the house, running errands, and other "stuff" to fill the time. But I did *not* spend time reflecting or sitting by myself in silence listening to the voice of God.

You know, I just don't like myself that much to be in silence with my thoughts. Just kidding, but I think most of you understand what I am saying. The first thing I do when I get into a quiet house or car is turn on the TV or Relevant Radio. Silence scares me.

At the next meeting with my coach, he asked me about my reflection time. I told him I didn't really do that very much, *but* I was committed to doing it the following week.

I continued to go to daily Mass the following week as well. My first day at daily Mass was at St. John the Baptist and I sat in the back. I didn't sit in my usual seat in the front right like I do on Sunday morning. I am not sure why, perhaps because this is a different and much smaller group of people. I felt a little bit like an outsider.

I really enjoy daily Mass and found it a blessing to have the Body of Christ in me every day. It makes me live more joyously and see the beauty in life and God in the small things like the sunrise, birds, and people I encounter throughout the day. I find that my smile is bigger and brighter, and I cannot wait to get out in the world and share my love. I am realizing the more I receive Him in the Eucharist, the more I feel Him take over my life.

After Mass, as I was walking out of the church, I stopped by a small Lighthouse CD stand to check it out. I haven't bought one in quite a while and the ones I have, I have listened to numerous times. As I stood there, a woman came up to me and said, "You should check out that one," pointing to another table. We started to talk about my addiction to the CDs.

She introduced herself, and we chatted for about five minutes. She mentioned she was part of a woman's prayer group, I said, "You know, I should pay it forward, come to my car, and I will give you a stack of these you can share them with the ladies." I think I gave her a couple dozen CDs.

And as I was doing that I couldn't help but feel sad. I didn't want to part with the CDs but I felt I was helping to evangelize, and I could always get more. She was very grateful and I hope that somehow, I was the laborer for the Lord by sacrificing my own selfish wants to keep them for myself. I once read on a bumper sticker, "Keep the Faith—But Not to Yourself." Brilliant!

We also talked about the fact that I felt weird following along with the readings on my smartphone. I said I hope nobody thinks I am browsing the web or texting. I asked how she followed along and she said she had a book.

I asked, "Have you heard about Carpeverbum?"

She had no idea what I was talking about. I pulled out my phone, showed her the text that I get daily and clicked the link. It takes you to USCCB (United States Conference of Catholic Bishops) website for the daily readings. It also has four sections to meditate on the meaning of the readings and helps you pray, listen and apply the teachings to your day.

It even has a daily screensaver, but I never have time to put that in place. They are beautiful pictures and lovely quotes to remind you how to live out the Gospel for that day. Perhaps I should add that to my list?

Think about it, how many times do you pick up your phone and check it? If I had to see a Gospel quote or a reminder how to live the Gospel 50 plus times a day, I am pretty sure it would impact my actions and how I interacted with people. Okay, it is going on the list.

I wrote down the number to text on her business card, and I hope she did sign up so she can have daily reminders on her phone, first thing when she gets up! I can't imagine carrying around another book. There are so many tools we can use on our devices!

The next day before Mass started, Father Jacek walked up the center aisle, and he stopped to say, "I am so happy to see you at daily Mass!"

I thought to myself, "Uh, you know who I am? Really?"

I was quite shocked. I replied, "I only started this week." He responded, "At least you started, I am so happy to see you."

I can't quite remember exactly what he said because I was beside myself that he knew who I was and that he stopped to talk to me.

This is not helping with my anonymity and keeping to myself.

Does he also see me slither out the door on Sunday, too? Ouch. But that was quickly overshadowed by the loving welcome and feeling of 'family' I felt by his few words and his touch on my arm. Yep, he's a "toucher" too.

I told Jeff when he got home. I was shocked that he knew who I was, he didn't know my name, but the woman who comes with no makeup and hair in a ponytail and sits in the front on the right.

Uh oh, I feel this camaraderie building and this community/family thing that Jesus really wanted for us as we come together to worship Him. I am pretty sure he doesn't want us to sit in the corner and be anti-social like I have been.

The following day I decided to go sit in my Sunday spot up in the front on the right.

I walked in with a couple who go to Sunday Mass with me. They are a cute couple and very faith-based. They looked like they attend daily Mass as well since they have been there every day with me that week. They have a daughter with a son who joins them some Sundays.

They are so cute; he and she hug and cuddle most of the Mass. I also saw that the wife helps administer Communion to those who cannot attend Mass. I am thinking that would be something I would be interested in while I have the time as I am in "transition" determining my professional vocation. They call it an Extraordinary Eucharistic Minister.

Add that to the list!

As we departed Mass, we walked out together. By the car, she asked, "What is your name, we see you all the time?" I confess that I had only been going to daily Mass for a few days and I introduced myself.

God is definitely showing me that church is a community and helping our fellow parishioners while we worship Him is what he expects from us.

19

How Do I Discern My Vocation?

This is not easy. We all struggle with our own self-doubting thoughts not to mention battling all that comes from the Evil One. He works hard on me, and I am doing my best to renounce him in Jesus' name, but I need to be more diligent about that and rely on the Lord to be with me every day, every moment, every thought.

This is so difficult.

Guess what? In true form, I am hearing about discerning vocations on the radio and in some the readings. I cannot express enough how odd but yet how normal it is to hear just what I need to hear right when I need to hear it. It is God speaking throughout the day, and I am training myself to see and hear Him in everything because he is communicating with me *always*.

When I first started to think about what my calling was in this world, I saw signs everywhere. Thank goodness, the Lord cleared my eyes and ears so when they were put in my way I saw and heard them where I was. There were times when I laughed out loud in my car and said, "Haaaaa, God, I hear you, I do!"

One thing that has helped me is going through this process with my coach. Figuring out the "why" and seeing if it matches my "how" which are my natural talents and then determining the "what" which are the jobs I should look at to fulfill my "why."

In the beginning, this sounded like a bunch of foo-foo crap to me. Let me just find a job that I think fulfills what I am called to do. I can figure it out from there. But I was no closer to figuring that out, and frankly, I was less and less confident that I could explain to anyone what I felt I was called to do.

When we first started our sessions, I wanted everything to be done in a month. I wanted to know the project plan, what steps we were going to take when I could expect an outcome and to understand the complete process from beginning to end. It was more than frustrating when my coach told me that it doesn't work that way. That each person is different. While there is a process, it is not like the project plans that I have been managing in my IT career where you report on status and progress each week. It is very iterative, and my journey is unique to me.

This was frustrating, to say the least. At the beginning of our sessions, I was such a mess. Our first session I was so emotional. I was scared, and I was concerned about what everyone would think of me going through this "process." I was in a fog. Clearly, I was more freaked out about everything than I thought. My coach said it was a great session.

WHAT?

He said it was good to let this release happen and it will help unblock me moving forward. I was EXHAUSTED after that call. He told me to do nothing for the rest of the day, go for a walk, take in some nature, and don't think much about it. He gave me some homework, and we met the following week.

Each week, I was in a good place, then bad place, then good place, then bad place. But each time I met with my coach I felt like he picked me up and put me back on the tracks, even when I was in a bad place *ten minutes* before our call. I just wanted this "thing" to be over and to get on with my life. I now know that it is not *my* time but *God's* time, which is why I needed to stop and slow down to *listen* and *feel.*

I continued to work with my coach. The first four weeks wrapped up, and we began another four because I was not quite there yet. This was much more difficult than I thought.

One day I was listening to The Drew Mariani Show at 3:00 during his Divine Mercy Chaplet. Drew recites this prayer with his audience every single day. People can call in, and hundreds of thousands of people pray for their intentions. Some call in for sickness, some for prayers to find a job, some with relationship problems, faith conversions, etc.

I would like to encourage you to do your own research on Saint Faustina and her encounter with Jesus and Divine Mercy. It changed my life, and I try to listen to Drew as often as I can so I can pray for the people who dearly need God's mercy! And let's not forget that Divine Mercy Sunday, put in place by St. John Paul II, was my first confession after 26 years. I feel as if *I* was a direct recipient of Jesus' Divine Mercy.

I called into Drew's show because I could use a few hundred thousand or so prayers for me, too! I felt guilty, I have to admit. People were calling about REAL tragedies such as babies fighting for their lives, mothers with no money in their bank account unable to feed their children, cancer sufferers, natural disaster survivors, shooting victims and people in their last hours of life!

And I am going to call in to have people pray for me to discern my professional vocation?

Really?

But I also know that others are fighting this battle themselves as well. When someone calls in with an issue, Drew turns it into ALL people who are struggling with that problem. So, he would throw it out for anyone who is discerning their professional vocations.

The one thing I do know is MANY people are going through transitions in their lives. At a certain point, some people say, "Is *this* what I was created to do?" The more people I network with, the more I find this to be true. And it is so sad that most people are finding this out in their 40's and 50's. What if we discerned our professional vocation as young adults, through the eyes of our faith, before we took our first job? I think our world would be drastically different.

It is probably not a surprise that I have Relevant Radio in my contact list. I quickly dialed and hoped that I was one of the lucky three or four callers. Winner, winner, chicken dinner, the sweet producer picks up the phone and says, "Welcome to the Drew Mariani Show, are you calling to be on the Chaplet?" I joyously respond with, "Yes I am!"

When I got on with Drew, I explained that I was in transition and felt the pull to do what I have always done, *not* what I felt I am called to do. I also slid in a conversion request for my husband, telling him that I believe he just wants me to get a job and get on with it. *I* have faith, *him*, not so much.

Drew began to laugh. He totally got it and shared with the audience that he, too, was just talking with his daughter about discerning what she wants to do as she moves into the workforce.

I hung up the phone so grateful that I could get others to pray for *all* the people who are discerning their professional vocations, myself included, of course.

This morning the Gospel was *Luke 10: 1-12*. The time is now for us to evangelize, not tomorrow, not next week. The Lord needs us to save others *today*. But there are very few of us out there willing to evangelize.

> The harvest is abundant, but the laborers are few.

So many people could use the saving grace of faith and God in their lives. There are just not a whole lot of people out there doing just that—evangelizing and helping others find it! Is this what I am called to do?

I continued to work through the process with my coach, and regardless of my ultimate decision on a career path, I felt the need to write this book now because it has been tugging at me for the past two years.

Am I crystal clear on my purpose at this time? Almost.

Can I articulate with passion to anyone who asks me? For the most part, I think. If I can just quiet my own thoughts in my own head, my doubts, my fears, my insecurities.

20

Be Still and Listen

Remember me saying that I don't really like myself enough to be with my thoughts very long? Well, come to find out, I have really enjoyed the silence. It is still hard for me to do it, but I am getting much better at it and need to do it more often and *longer*.

This past week was my test to myself to see if I could really commit to putting God first and listening to what He is saying to me. This means in silence, in Scripture, in prayer, or on the radio. I need to be open to all the signs He is giving me and seek Him in everything throughout the day.

My goal was to get up at 5:00 with Jeff, make his lunch and send him on his way to work. I would NOT go back to bed—I would stay up, read the daily readings, read Carpeverbum, listen to "In Conversation with God" and the pray the rosary on Relevant Radio app. My reflection time would happen while I watched the sunrise and then off to Mass I would go. Some mornings I would also pray the rosary at church or stay after for some time in Adoration.

The mornings are SO peaceful now. I look forward the peace and quiet to center me every day, and now I pay attention to the beauty of starting the day with the animals, birds, geese, and ducks. I have also been in silence during the day, in the midst of the madness, just to stop and ask for God to help me. Silence is unfamiliar to most of us, and I am finding it is necessary for our soul. And when you hear Him talking to you, and you know it, you thirst for the silence, you need it to live, just like water.

Every single day this week I have come home and poured my heart into this book. That means me, my computer, and nothing else except my dog. I sit in silence all day long while I try to compile my thoughts to share an entertaining, informative, and hopefully inspiring testimony of how faith and a relationship with God will enrich your life.

I almost went back to bed Thursday morning this week. But my other goal, in addition to putting God first and reflecting, is to have a manuscript completed so I can give it to Father Rocky this Saturday morning at the McHenry County Prayer Breakfast!

Who does stuff like this to themselves?

I am not a professional writer. What made me think I could crank out a book in *5 days*?

I am a procrastinator, though! I work best under pressure.

I CAN DO IT!

I think I can, I think I can, I think I can ... O Holy Spirit, Mary, and Jesus, please, please, please help me!

21

Faith—it is a Journey—NOT a Destination

If I can impart one thing to everyone, it is that faith is a journey. It is never-ending. You don't arrive until you pass from this earth and arrive at your final destination, Heaven.

Queue the angelic music now.

God has been working deep in my soul for my entire life, but I just wasn't listening or paying attention. Maybe I couldn't have cared less about what God wanted because my life was fabulous. It could have been because I had a swimmer's ear numerous times when I was younger and that is how all the wax built up in there.

Kidding, of course.

I know that each and every day I learn something new about myself, my situation, my family, or my faith. He met me and continues to meet me every day, where I am! He will meet you, too! I hear this from people God puts in my way, resources of all forms and my yearning to grow in faith, hope and love. The more I learn, the less I can turn away.

Even though it was "all about me" in the beginning, I now realize it is "all about us."

The secular world we live in is stifling God. I have no clue why He blessed me with the grace and gift of yearning for what Catholicism means and why I should live according to its teachings. All I know is how grateful I am that I was given the grace to hear it and that I will try my best to understand and live it. And hopefully, people will see that in me and want it for themselves.

I see myself slowly changing. I am slowly getting it. And I will never arrive adequately knowledgeable and faithful until I am purified in Purgatory or in Heaven. I will continue to learn, make mistakes, pick myself back up and ask for forgiveness under the church's perfectly-defined commandments and sacraments.

I now understand that God made these rules, not to frustrate us, but to help us live joyous and righteous lives, He gave us a clear map to His Kingdom. I still need to grow and learn. It is not just about making ME more holy. I am called to be a disciple of Jesus, and that means ensuring I am living the Gospel myself *plus* introducing Jesus to others. This means I need to simply communicate why I am Catholic; I can always improve in these areas.

One of the tools I signed up for is an online course, ClaritasU. It helps address the topics where I am struggling to explain or defend my beliefs, *with love*. The primary purpose is to help people explain the faith and why we believe all that the Catholic Church teaches. I think it is a great resource and would like to thank Brandon Vogt and Bishop Robert Barron for their vision. Brandon recently came out with a book, *Why I am Catholic (And You Should Be Too)*. ADD TO LIST!

I hope to be super confident and armed with the knowledge and conviction to ROAR about Catholicism, knowing that I will have to carry my cross as there are so many people who are not open to faith and Catholicism in particular. I need to share the peace and joy that I have experienced through the blessings of the sacraments that are offered in the Catholic Faith and how building a relationship with Jesus is paramount to living a fruitful life.

I need to inspire others to enrich their lives through faith and prayer. You will have a more personally rewarding and professionally successful life when you view everything through the lens of your faith, *everything* is richer with God.

Afterword

I hope to help every "Joe" and "Joann" with my real-life story of someone who had it all and didn't really need God. Life was good. Actually, it was awesome! Or so I thought.

Once I did find my faith, I was amazed at how much more enriched and enlightened my worldview became. My faith has impacted *every* aspect of my life positively. Most important was how I was able to deal with the trials that came my way and how I had the humility to give it *all* up to God and let Him show me the good in everything.

I share my struggle with faith, humility and surrendering to God. I share how I battled to discern my next professional vocation and what I decided for the next chapter of my life.

I have an overwhelming sense of peace knowing that God has a plan and that I just need to listen by spending time reflecting in silence and in prayer and trust in Him completely. My compassion towards people has grown exponentially. I want to inspire people to enrich their lives through faith and prayer; to live with compassion, forgiveness and let faith be the lens to your world leading to a more personally rewarding and professionally successful life.

I have told my story numerous times to friends, colleagues, family members, people I just met on the plane and in airports or at parties. I think people are intrigued by my faith and frankly, might just be looking for some more meaning to this life or for the joy I radiate when I share my journey with them.

Perhaps that answer lies in God?

Enjoy the honest and raw read my heart and soul are out there for you all to see!

I hope to be a Sherpa to others on their journey through my experience and research perhaps catapulting you forward to build your own unique relationship with God and to a life with meaning, joy, and peace.

Please check out my website "my digital soul" for more free resources to help you!

www.kendravonesh.com

- Navigate your early journey with steps on how to go back to the church
- Resource guide of apps, radio, TV, websites, books, CDs, movies

- Vlogs and blogs—ways to help you look through the lens of faith in your daily lives! I promise not to be over the top, and I what I share *will* impact your life. If you are interested, I go deep into my reasons why I came to believe and love all that is the Catholic faith.

I also created *The Compassionate Culture* to bring spiritual souls together aching for more joy, kindness and love in their lives. Sign up for the exclusive community today!

www.kendravonesh.com/compassionate-culture

I am here to serve YOU! Please send me your candid feedback on this book, other ideas you have for the website or anything you would like me to develop to enrich your life through faith, prayer and a relationship with God.

kendra@kendravonesh.com

May God bless you ALWAYS!

The List

I wasn't kidding when I told you I have a lot to learn and that I keep a list of things that will help me on my journey. Let's recollect what I said I need to do in case you were keeping track! If you have anything for me to add to this list, please let me know, I am always looking for help. Lord knows I need it!

- Commit to my next chapter in life. Passionately articulate what my purpose and meaning is on this earth—my professional vocation—without letting fear rule my life

- Putting God first every day and throughout the day. Trust in Jesus—"pray, trust, and don't worry" live his words, "Do not fear" go to daily mass, time in silence, reflection and Adoration

- Meet with a Spiritual Director

- Add Carbpeverbum screen saver to my smartphone to remind me of the daily readings and Gospel

- Be an Extraordinary Eucharistic Minister
- Improve my prayer life: reflect on my day, what I did good/not so good and where were God and the Devil working in my life at the end of every day
- Ask my family to watch "The Case for Christ" movie with me
- Read The Old Testament, preferably in my new paper Bible I haven't cracked open yet
- Read the *Compendium and Catechism of the Catholic Church*
- Read *Why I am Catholic (And You Should Be Too)*
- Do the walking tour at the Maximilian Kolbe Shrine and the Heavenly walk
- Figure out a way to go to Mass with my mom
- Volunteer
- Say grace before meals
- Go back to the ClaritasU lessons so I can better explain why I am Catholic

Epilogue

I have chipped away at my list!

I have increased my time in prayer, reflection, and silence. I *try* to start my day with reading the scriptures and some reflections on their meaning and how they are speaking to me each day. I also *try* to go to Mass every day because I *feel* God taking over when I receive Him in the Eucharist. I need Him to guide me because I have no clue what I am doing. I am NOT perfect with daily Mass, prayers, or reflection, but I work on it every day. All I know is when I start my day with God those are the most peaceful and joyous days.

I volunteered for the McHenry County Prayer Breakfast Committee and have met some fabulous spiritual warriors who are now true friends. One of them invited me to a Cenacle prayer group on Thursday mornings after Mass, and I have attended a couple of times. It is a pretty intense couple of hours, and the people in the group are more than inspiring to me with their kindness, love and faith. They opened their hearts to me and they are already asking how to help with my mission! I am so blessed.

Because I am going to Mass more frequently, I am also going to confession more often so that I am in the best state when I receive Him. I *love* confession, what a gift and I am taking advantage of that sacrament as often as I can. I am much more aware of how I am living and what my actions are doing to my soul, life and professional vocation. I try to go at least two times a month, if not more. This is not me bragging or boasting, I am honestly humbled by my sinful ways and need to ask for forgiveness, so He can best work through me to help me make this world a better place to live.

I have become humbler over these past few months, which is a *very* different way of living for me. I have surrendered myself to God and handed Him the wheel so He can lead me down the best path for this unforeseen and uncharted journey. Humility is incredibly important as I move into this new, unfamiliar, scary and exciting time of my life.

What is that new life, you ask?

I have decided to leave my executive career in corporate America to inspire others to enrich their lives through faith and prayer. I am going out on my own to share with the world how faith has transformed me and to help others lead a more personally rewarding and professionally successful life through a relationship with God and the beautiful gifts of Catholicism.

God is amazing as he keeps putting people in my way to help me. Along with publishing this book, I am working on a website (my digital soul), The Compassionate Culture community, vlogs, blogs, speaking engagements and I owe this all to my book "Sherpa" Angie. She is a Godsend and props to Sima who has helped me with my personal branding and messaging. Let's not forget Jeff Baker my life coach and dear friend! They have been instrumental in helping me swim through the murky waters and have been so patient with me as I paddle about in circles sometimes.

What else did I accomplish on my list?

I became good friends with Father Jacek who has become one of my biggest fans and supporters. I also found a Spiritual Director, Father Caliente, who is helping me along my journey to ensure I keep my hand in God's and for Him to guide me. We have only met two times and I cannot wait to see where this all goes. I recently met Father Parker who is a force, for sure, and who bestows blessings on me and prays for me more than I deserve. All the women who support these priests and the parish have been awesome, there are too many to name, unfortunately.

I completed the Heavenly walk at the Shrine as I contemplated my new professional vocation. I have revisited lessons on ClaritasU to help me with my blogs and vlogs and still need to complete more, but it is a start.

My family watched "The Case for Christ" with me on Christmas Day. It was great to have them watch the movie with me, even if they may have found it painful. I am not so sure it converted or was an epiphany for anyone, but I wanted them to see Jesus from a different perspective. Anyone who doesn't believe in Jesus must watch this Atheist couple convert! Spoiler alert—the husband, who was a Chicago Tribune reporter was trying to prove, through facts and research, that Jesus didn't exist. He failed miserably at his attempt and eventually became a believer and is now a pastor and author of many Jesus books, Lee Strobel.

Both boys are now living with us full time along with their dogs, it is awesome! I am so blessed and so excited about all the changes that are coming our way as a family. It is the fourth Sunday of Lent, 2018, as I finish this book. I am renewing my dedication to sacrifice and prayer for these 40 days because I sense a tangible renewal of my life both personally and professionally. I am very excited for Easter and Spring which I hope brings us prosperity and many blessings. I gave up alcohol for Lent this year instead of volunteering—so far so good. I am finding out that starting your own business is extremely time-consuming and it is not an 8:00-5:00 job whatsoever. The less I drink, the more energy and focus I have to continue to make progress on my new professional vocation and faith mission.

From the C-Suite to God's Suite!

I was the testimonial speaker at Relevant Radio's Lenten Luncheon in Oak Brook Terrace in March and have been blessed with a few Relevant Radio spots to promote this book. Thank you to Father Rocky for passing my manuscript along to Linda Ruf and Carol Tomaselli. Those two women are amazing Catholic souls and continue to be my sisters in Christ!

I also spoke about my journey at St. Mary's prior to Susan Tassone's presentation and had a fabulous evening as Lenten speaker at Holy Cross in Batavia where I met some "on fire" parishioners including Mark Middendorf, one of the founders of Lighthouse Catholic Media. He gave me a book to pass along to Jeff. We shall see if it goes on HIS list!

Speaking of which, my husband has been more than supportive helping with all aspects of my new mission including videos, photography and creative input on the website and book. He has even attended a Legatus Chicago Chapter dinner with me where we met many Catholic business owners and executives including Dave Durand and his awesome wife Tammy and Patrick McCaskey, grandson of the Chicago Bear's founder George Halas. The faith of all these professionals is remarkable and what great people they are.

I am also jazzed about how many people have joined The Compassionate Culture community already and I hope to inspire people far and wide to *Lead with Compassion.*

Remember, God will meet you *where you are*, you just have to invite Him! He will do the rest and I hope to be of some help as you journey through this life with meaning, joy and peace—hand in hand with Jesus!

I will leave you with a bible verse from someone who didn't think she needed God! I had it all, everything I wanted in this world—or did I—and would I *want* God and want to *change*? It has only been five years, I cannot wait to see how God uses me to help make this world a better place in the years to come!

GOD BLESS YOU!

1 Timothy 6: 3-10

> Whoever teaches something different and
> does not agree with the sound words of our
> Lord Jesus Christ and the religious teaching
> is conceited, understanding nothing, and has a
> morbid disposition for arguments and verbal
> disputes. From these come envy, rivalry, insults,
> evil suspicions, and mutual friction among
> people with corrupted minds, who are deprived
> of the truth, supposing religion to be a means
> of gain. Indeed, religion with contentment
> is a great gain. For we brought nothing into
> the world, just as we shall not be able to take

anything out of it. If we have food and clothing, we shall be content with that. Those who want to be rich are falling into temptation and into a trap and into many foolish and harmful desires, which plunge them into ruin and destruction. For the love of money is the root of all evils, and some people in their desire for it have strayed from the faith and have pierced themselves with many pains.

About the Author

Kendra Von Esh was all about money and prestige. She quickly climbed the corporate ladder and took advantage of all the comforts this world had to offer. It wasn't until she began to focus on a diet to cleanse her body that she realized she had yet to cleanse her soul.

A non-practicing Catholic, Kendra didn't know much of anything about her faith and did not go to church. She didn't think she needed God because her life was great the way it was … until the Holy Spirit got a hold of her. After attending Mass on Easter Sunday in 2013, there was no stopping her.

After years of research, struggle, and hilarious misadventures, Kendra now fully understands why the Catholic Church has the sacraments and commandments—and why everyone should live the way of the full and only church brought to us by Jesus Christ.

Kendra is definitely a work-in-progress. But after leaving her high-powered corporate career behind, she has recommitted her life to living her faith and inspiring others to enrich their lives through faith and prayer.

Bonus: Resource Guide

Unsure of where to begin on your own spiritual journey? Wondering what tools, CDs, DVDs, and books Kendra recommends?

Download the *Welcome Home! Resource Guide* and meet God where you are today!

https://kendravonesh.com/guide

CPSIA information can be obtained
at www.ICGtesting.com
Printed in the USA
FFHW011604301119
56470698-62278FF